UNLOCKING THE
DOOR TO
**EXCELLENT GRADES**
AT THE
**COLLEGE AND
UNIVERSITY LEVEL**

# UNLOCKING THE DOOR TO
# EXCELLENT GRADES
## AT THE
# COLLEGE AND UNIVERSITY LEVEL

## MOSES N.B. AYIKU JR.

 iUniverse®

# UNLOCKING THE DOOR TO EXCELLENT GRADES AT THE COLLEGE AND UNIVERSITY LEVEL

*iUniverse books may be ordered through booksellers or by contacting:*

*iUniverse*
*1663 Liberty Drive*
*Bloomington, IN 47403*
*www.iuniverse.com*
*1-800-Authors (1-800-288-4677)*

*Because of the dynamic nature of the Internet, any web addresses or links contained in this book may have changed since publication and may no longer be valid. The views expressed in this work are solely those of the author and do not necessarily reflect the views of the publisher, and the publisher hereby disclaims any responsibility for them.*

*Any people depicted in stock imagery provided by Getty Images are models, and such images are being used for illustrative purposes only. Certain stock imagery © Getty Images.*

*ISBN: 978-1-5320-7147-8 (sc)*
*ISBN: 978-1-5320-7148-5 (e)*

*Print information available on the last page.*

*iUniverse rev. date:  08/15/2019*

# About the Author

Moses N.B. Ayiku Jr. was born in Ghana, West Africa. Moses grew up in the US in the 1970's before returning to Ghana to continue his education. He relocated to the United States in 2002 and has since worked on Wall Street and been an adjunct faculty at seven colleges and universities in the U.S. Moses is the former Manager of the Small Business Development Center (SBDC) at Seminole State College in Sanford, Florida. He completed the Spring 2019 semester as an Adjunct faculty at Seminole State College. The course he taught was Economics. Moses is a graduate of the Rutgers Business School and the University of Ghana, Legon.

# Contents

# Preface

In the past fifteen years my work as an adjunct faculty at several colleges and universities in New Jersey, New York, Connecticut and Florida has been very illuminating. During discussions about various business topics with my students, there are often questions that fall into the domain of the learning process. My students often ask questions about how they can improve their academic performance. Over the years, such questions compelled me to prepare auxiliary materials as handouts for them. The honest feedback from students concerning these handouts and presentations enabled me to continue to modify and enhance the materials.

During one of the occasions when I was asked questions about strategies for balancing school with work a suggestion was made; that it would be helpful to many students if I were to compile my materials into a book. Quite a number of students have the daunting task of being full time students, working full time and also having an array of private commitments. Others may be in school (and do not work) but still want to know all they can on how they can improve their academic performance. This book is for all such students; those who want to elevate their grades and are prepared to put in the work.

I found useful information about study techniques and time management as a student myself, speaking with other students as well as reading various books about learning strategies, time management and other related topics. In addition, fifteen years of teaching, discussing and sharing study techniques with students has also enabled me to build up a dossier of ideas that work.

Perhaps there are students out there who have questions and want simple answers to them; mainly about how to excel in school or at the university level. I have put together materials that I am sure will answer many of those questions. It is my hope that by writing this book I can assist students to fulfill their academic goals.

The material I have provided is especially geared towards social science and business students. For me, it is an opportunity to share some of the lessons I have learnt over a period of time spanning over thirty years; initially as a student and now as an instructor. The experiences I have had coupled with the various surveys and research assignments that I have conducted with students have all been tremendous sources of valuable insights. This book should be able to assist anyone entering the college or university level to appreciate some important steps towards ensuring academic success, something every student should be aiming for.

Education is the singular most important investment one can ever make. Our world is a better place every day that someone graduates from one academic institution or other. Let us hope that as a society, we will have the will power to not sit on our laurels but continue to enhance the educational experience for new generations to come.

This book is dedicated to all those students who asked me thought provoking questions over the years that compelled me to draw deep to provide quality responses.

# 1.0

# Introduction

"When you're finished changing, you're finished."
Benjamin Franklin

Being a student in a college or university comes with a certain amount of stress, regardless of the particular situation that you are in. There are a lot of assignments to be completed, exams to be written and group projects with challenging classmates. In addition to all these activities, many students have to grapple with other issues such as stretching their limited finances, working during school, managing relationships with family and friends as well as keeping some form of social life going.

With all the above challenges, is it possible for students to do well, perhaps even excel in college? The answer is a definite yes! Yes, you can do well in college regardless of the above challenges. You can take care of school work, excel in school and still have a life!

How does one go about ensuring that one does very well in college? For the most part it takes effective planning. Manage your time and know what your priorities are at each and every stage. In addition, you must hanker for high grades and desire them so strongly that you are prepared to go the extra mile to get them. Those who are able to combine working hard with working smart truly do get rewarded. Your academic success will be determined to a large extent on how well you utilize your time.

This book provides specific guidelines geared towards enabling you to excel in college and boost your grades. The most interesting thing about the information I have gathered is that some of the suggestions, advice and strategies seem so simple! Sometimes the answers to our problems do not have to be complicated.

In the past fifteen plus years, I have worked with various institutions of higher learning as an adjunct faculty. I started out as an English Tutor. The students who came for tutoring needed more than a review of their essays and English grammar. Many of them wanted to do well in school, but they lacked basic study skills. These students put in a lot of effort and were clearly frustrated that their efforts were not getting the desired results. I offered my assistance to a number of these students in developing study plans and strategies. Those who followed their study plans had strong and positive results; many of them were excited with the tremendous improvements in their GPA's! That is exactly what they were looking for! For the remainder of the semester, I could see the increase in confidence in these students. They definitely felt empowered and capable. Their secret to success was effective planning and improved time management.

When I started teaching, I found the need to share exam strategies and other aspects of the learning process with a number of my students. We would discuss different methods of studying and strategies that they could easily implement to improve their academic performance. Over 1,000 college/university students have passed through my hands in the past fifteen years. My goal was to share with these student's methods they could adapt to suit their own particular learning styles. This book is as a result of my experiences in the academic world as a student and as an instructor with these students.

This book is about providing strategies that will enable you to improve your academic behavior and motivate you to do the best that you can. The number of hours that you spend studying definitely plays a role in determining your overall academic performance. However, take note that it is the quality of those hours that actually does the trick in terms of moving you from a B grade to an A grade. That is where both planning and effective time management come into play.

To get the most out of this book, I suggest that you utilize the material presented like a menu and select the options that would work best for you. Make modifications and adjustments that will suit your particular lifestyle and learning approach. However, remember that a majority of the information provided is supported by the actual performance of top students in a number of institutions of higher learning. The methods have been tried and tested and you will gain by introducing them into your study plan.

Obtaining a degree means you are trying to enhance your value on the labor market. The degree is a strategic input that you want to acquire to obtain that job which may very well be the beginning of an exciting career. Prepare your own SWOT Analysis (Strengths, Weaknesses, Opportunities and Threats) and Study Plan to achieve the highest grades possible. In addition, make time to research your possible career direction to ensure that your academic efforts are in tandem with your career goals. Make sure that you align all efforts to achieve not only academic but professional success as well. Chapter 2 will provide more information about preparing your study plan and undertaking your individual SWOT Analysis.

In the ensuing chapters, you will be given an overview of the overall academic process. Understanding the academic process is central to developing a strategy to getting excellent grades. One must first of all understand the environment. Next, specific steps are highlighted that will provide a direct map to getting the highest grades possible.

Each chapter focuses on specific aspects of the academic process from exams, math challenges, time management, stress management, writing quality reports and making great presentations. Read each chapter with the intention of picking up specific steps that you can add to your existing arsenal. Remember, you are looking for ways to improve what you are doing now. There may be many things that you are doing properly already. The aim of this book is to take you to the next level in terms of higher grades. If you are now planning to start a degree program, then this book presents an opportunity to review and find out the options that are available to you as far as learning strategies and academic success. The earlier you start looking at strategies, the greater the chance of success.

A chapter is devoted towards the use of current technologies to support academic efforts. In my estimation, we underutilize many of the existing technologies even as we continue to yearn for newer technologies! Technology opens up new alternatives and approaches; it is important to embrace these to your benefit. Be creative and find new ways to adapt existing technologies to your advantage. With the advent of smart phones, tablets, apps and notebooks, there are many options that can be utilized to enhance academic progress. You do not have to have the fanciest devices, but you can use the devices you have to modernize your approach to learning.

A special introduction exercise has been placed in Appendix 1a and 1b. Called the Education Success Profile (E.S.P.), it is a series of questions that you are encouraged to answer honestly and grade before you continue reading the rest of this book. The responses will enable you to identify and focus on the areas that you need to strengthen in order to excel in your academic journey. The interpretation of your results as well as basic steps to rectify challenging areas has been outlined in Appendix 1b.

The book has been written in a simple and straight forward manner to ensure that the material is as self-explanatory as possible. Any unique terms and concepts are clearly defined to avoid any confusion. Diagrams and appendices are used to further emphasizes specific points. Special reference is made to websites that can provide additional information on particular topics and sub-topics. Key steps are clearly outlined and this will make them easy to follow. The steps come along with detailed explanations within the text.

It is my hope that each student that reads this book would be able to identify strategies that they can implement on their own to achieve tremendous academic success by uncapping the potential for success that each of us has within us. If you want to attain excellent grades, then the time to start working is now! Outline your goals, put in the work and expect the results!

**Serene Campus View**

"Never leave that till tomorrow which you can do today." Benjamin Franklin

# 2.0

# The Study Plan

"Do not fear mistakes. You will know failure. Continue to reach out."
Benjamin Franklin

The first step in organizing yourself for a good academic semester is to develop a good study plan. This plan should tell you what you should be doing on any particular day at any time. The study plan is a calendar of all your key activities while in school. The study plan should take all of the following into consideration:

- Course outlines/textbooks/e-books, reference materials/news etc./other course materials
- Course requirements/assignments/projects/exams/presentations
- Course/Non Course relationships/faculty/seniors/classmates/other relationships (family/friends)
- Time management/academic deadlines/class schedule/study periods/rest periods/ socialization periods

By carefully placing the right emphasis on all of the above, you will be able to develop a study plan that can guide you to success. The important thing is to make sure your study plan is actually followed! Your academic success will depend on developing a good study plan and following it as much as possible. Your aim should be to get the highest grades possible. When you put in the right quantity and quality of work, you will see positive results.

To get started, it is important to first understand the basic learning process. An overall view of the learning process will give us the ability to appreciate the focus on different activities within the academic setting. Following is a diagram showing the overall academic process. All the activities/items feed into your final grade.

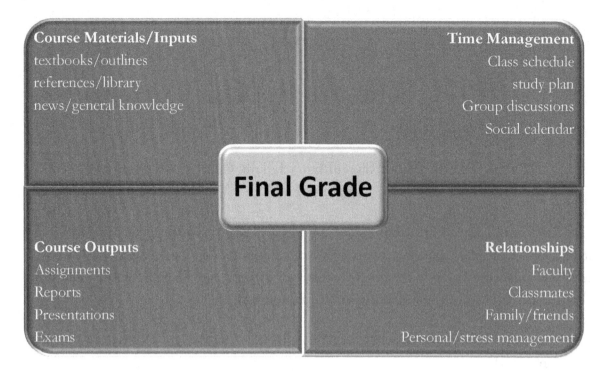

**Course Materials/Inputs**
textbooks/outlines
references/library
news/general knowledge

**Time Management**
Class schedule
study plan
Group discussions
Social calendar

**Final Grade**

**Course Outputs**
Assignments
Reports
Presentations
Exams

**Relationships**
Faculty
Classmates
Family/friends
Personal/stress management

**The Academic Process Simplified**

## 2.1 Course Outlines/Materials

These days, most course outlines/information are available online through various learning management systems such as blackboard or canvas. It may be helpful to organize yourself by printing out the relevant course outlines and other materials for each course and placing them in well-organized folders. Become familiar with the course outline, extra handouts, projects, assignments, deadlines as well as exam information. All this information should be noted and put in your study plan. For example, any exam dates should be noted in your study plan. Other important dates such as deadlines for submitting assignments/projects and other academic outputs should all be clearly noted within your study plan. This will enable you to keep track of all requirements and ensure that you always submit your work on time. The impact of timely submissions will be less stress as well as the possibility of attaining maximum possible grades as one avoids penalties that may arise from late submissions. The course outline is clearly one of the most important documents for every student to thoroughly review. One must ensure that there is full understanding of its contents. Any areas that are not clear should be discussed with your professor. This exercise would ensure that you start your academic campaign on the right foot; knowing what exactly is expected of you during the semester, for any given course.

Opening up folders for each course will assist you to remain organized and place relevant course information in their respective folders. In doing so, your course materials will be well organized and easy to find. Further, as the semester rolls on you will be able to add to each folder as assignments and other projects are completed. As exams approach, these well-organized folders will be your resource base that will help in your preparation.

## 2.2 Books for the Course

The list of required textbooks is usually indicated in the course outlines. Do everything possible to ensure that you have all your books on time to avoid delays in your learning process. Even if you don't have the book there are a number of credible options that you should investigate. The library may have a copy of the book. You could also find optional texts to use. Why not borrow someone's book for a couple of hours a week until you get yours? You could also try using Google. Many books have free chapters online; try searching for them. With the ISBN number, author(s) and title of the book you will be able to trace the book online and possibly unearth related materials that will be of benefit to you. A few minutes of extra research in the beginning of the semester can pay off tremendously in the form of better grades!

There are a number of websites such as Overstock.com which sell textbooks at reasonable prices. A number of students also utilize Amazon to buy their books. However, remember that ordering books through these websites might mean a period of having to manage your school work without the required text. Have a backup plan to ensure you do not lose out while waiting for the books to arrive. It is important to ensure that you obtain the right editions of the textbooks. For example, many textbooks have international editions; you have to compare the contents to make sure it is in line with the text that will be used in class. In recent times, students have informed me that not only do they buy used copies of textbooks using the internet, but they even rent books! With the advent of smart phones and tablets (including the IPAD), e-books are gaining in popularity. The advantage of an e-book is that you do not have a heavy load to carry. Pricewise, e-books are invariably more cost effective than the hard copies. Another advantage of e-books is the ability to read them with relative ease, whether you are on a subway, train or in a bus. Once you have all your books, remember that owning them is not the end of the task at hand. You must read them and make use of them on a regular basis!

For many courses, PowerPoint presentations are also made available to students. Be sure to use these as well. Ideally, printing out PowerPoint handouts will make your work easier. Typically, the PowerPoint is available on a chapter to chapter basis. If you have the printouts, you can take them to lectures and use them as your basis for writing notes. The printouts will save you time as well as allow a focus on understanding key points being explained by your Professors.

## 2.3 How do I use the Library?

Most schools provide seminars early in the semester on using the library. Take advantage of these programs to learn as much as possible about locating material in the library. Learn to use the library very well. Your ability to find the right material promptly will have a positive impact on your assignments and other academic activities. The librarians know where everything is; befriending them and asking questions will assist you greatly throughout your course. The library is a maze of information available to those who choose to use it. Save your time and improve your academic performance by learning how to use the library properly. Many schools have access to a variety of specialized databases through the school library. By virtue of being a student, one can obtain access to these rich sources of information. Make use of them as much as possible. It will improve the quality of your assignments as well as enhance your understanding of various topics and concepts as you read wide and learn more. With all these efforts, be clear that your response to exam questions will show that you have bothered to research effectively and learnt a variety of relevant issues on various topics.

## 2.4 Collecting Information: Using the Internet and other Sources of Information

The internet is perhaps the greatest information tool today. Learn how to effectively research and find information online. This is a very important skill that will assist you in your academic endeavors and save you time. The difference between good students and great students is that great students develop a knack for knowing where to find each type of information. Become familiar with core websites relevant for each course.

In searching for various pieces of information, use the keyword approach. Identify key words and phrases that are likely to lead you to the information you are looking for. Ask the popular questions such as why, what, where, how and when. When you are scanning your search results remember to stay focused on materials that are directly relevant to your initial search. Each search effort may provide millions of possible results. The most relevant search results are typically placed on top of the search list and you should focus on those. Be sure to modify your search terms and phrases to determine which brings you the most relevant search results. Be sure to catalogue the websites that you actually utilize as you may have to return to them at a later date. Also, noting your sources of information will make it easier to prepare a bibliography. In today's environment, online sources of information are becoming more and more relevant. Note your sources of information as they could come in handy for other assignments. In addition, it is important to credit your information sources by listing a detailed bibliography.

Be a collector of information. Make the effort to be broad minded by collecting information from various sources. Make it a habit to listen to the news regularly. Get access to magazines, journals and newspapers. Use your cell phone to get updates on news pieces. Acquire a radio that can provide current news and discussions on current issues. For many courses, a healthy understanding of current issues has a significant impact on academic progress. Make time for news gathering and if possible place it in your study plan as a regular event. This activity will pay off as you continue to improve your understanding of your environment. While you may choose to focus on specific news areas that are of interest to you, it is important to note relevant economic, business, political and social news. This gives you a broad based understanding of a diverse range of issues. You may not realize it, but as you continue to build up on your overall knowledge in the areas above, it has a positive impact on your academic work as well. For example, a business student who listens to business news regularly may have practical examples that they could discuss during exams. This kind of approach lets your Professor know that you understand the materials being taught and are well read. Once the examples are relevant, they will have a positive impact on the quality of your output as well as your grades.

## 2.5 Course Relationships: Who is Teaching the Course?

Does the choice you make of taking a class with one faculty over another matter? The answer is an emphatic yes! It is important to ask and find out who is teaching the course and what their style is. Each member of faculty has their own unique style. By researching on their approaches and respective styles you will be in a better position to determine whether you would be more comfortable with one faculty than another. Ratemyprofessors. com is one major source of information concerning faculty at all colleges and universities. Make sure to read as many comments as possible to get a fair view about the faculty. Some faculty members have outstanding reputations for supporting and guiding their students. That is what you should be looking for. If you want the most out of your school experience, then it is important to look out for faculty that will challenge you. A number of students look for faculty that they believe will give them an easy grade with minimal work. That is a wrong approach and the end result may not be to your satisfaction. Your overall focus when selecting courses should be based on more important factors such as the relevance to your area of specialization and future career choice. Selecting a course that others claim is easy may not bring you much in terms of your individual academic development. On the other hand, do not go to the other extreme and select the most difficult courses. Focus as mentioned earlier on the relevance of the course to your academic and professional goals. That should be your top priority.

## 2.6 Your Relationship with Faculty Members

Managing your relationship with all your professors is an important part of the academic process. Your professors are an excellent source of quality information and guidance. They can also serve as the ideal person to bounce ideas off. As a student, you have the right to arrange to meet your professor(s). Make appointments to meet with faculty when you have specific issues you need guidance or information on. Before going to such a meeting, show that you have initiative and undertake research on the issues you intend to raise. List your questions and make sure you have a clear focus for the meeting. This type of approach will get you the information you want as well as put you in a positive light. Positive relationships with your faculty create a level of goodwill that can be tapped to your advantage throughout your course and even after! A good relationship with a faculty member can mean a strong reference that can play a pivotal role in you getting that job you really want! Some professors even assist students with information and contacts concerning internships and other employment opportunities. Remember that you stand a chance of getting such information if you are known to the professors. An occasional sit down with your professors provides you with a great opportunity to network.

When meeting with faculty I suggested making appointments so that you can sit down and have a proper discussion. Many students approach faculty at what can only be described as the wrong times. The worst times to approach faculty for detailed discussions are just before or just after a lecture. Prior to a lecture a professor is focused on activities that will ensure that he/she is well prepared for the class. Immediately after a class, a professor may have another class and other commitments. Unless you are looking for very basic information, engaging your Professor in a discussion immediately after a class is not a good approach.

In terms of overall communication, make the effort to be a positive person with your faculty. They will remember you and it is in your interest to be remembered in a positive light. Goodwill is built up and you never know when you may have to cash in on the goodwill that you build up. At the end of the day your professors are human and everyone appreciates it when they are treated with respect!

## 2.7 Your Relationship with Seniors

If you are not sure of what courses to take, you can contact seniors (and professors) and ask them about particular courses you are interested in. Senior students who have undertaken those courses, and been through them successfully, can provide a wealth of information. Find out how they managed the course. What did they like/dislike about the course? What was their overall opinion about the course and why? This information can assist you in determining whether you want to take that course or not. If you decide to take that course, then the information would be helpful in planning how to succeed in that particular course. While this may seem disconcerting to some, develop the aptitude for introducing yourself and getting to know others, especially your seniors. It may initially seem awkward but with time you will develop the skill of interacting well with people by introducing yourself and engaging them in discussions on an array of issues. Further, networking is important and these interactions can be very beneficial to you as you continue your course. Seniors have gone through the mill and the valuable information that you obtain from them can save you a lot of grief as well as enable you to focus properly.

## 2.8  Study Buddies, Study Groups and Academic Alliances

It is beneficial to identify study partner(s) for every single course. Get to know your classmates and form strategic relationships with them. You can bounce ideas off them as well as share information on exams, projects and assignments. Networking with your course mates should start as soon as the semester begins. It will allow you to develop strong and positive relationships gradually as the semester unfolds. Having strategic alliances also enable you to have a pool of students that you can evolve and socialize with during the semester.

Shyness is the key enemy to fight in developing academic alliances on campus. Make the effort to network and obtain contact information and follow up on the phone numbers and email addresses. Do not wait until final exams to start contacting other students. You will be seen as a user and may not get the type of reception that you desire. Bonds are developed by sharing lunch and making adjustments to your schedule to spend time socializing with your classmates. Remember, the students you are in school with will form a major part of your network for the rest of your life. It is easier to cultivate these relationships while you are in school than after you have graduated. As I always tell my students, you will find it much easier trying to network amongst your class mates than with Jeff Bezos and Bill Gates!

You can and should form study groups. Make sure that you develop a clear agenda for these groups. Your study group should have specific members and each member should bring something to the table. Responsibilities should be well spread to ensure that everyone has an active role to play. Meeting times and places should be very specific. A dedication to attending all meetings well prepared will assist the whole group to achieve excellent results. I have met many students who indicated to me that success in their courses was partly due to the strong study groups that they formed.

## 2.9 Non Academic Relationships/Commitments

It is important to identify all your non-academic commitments. By taking account of these in your study plan, you end up having a well-rounded range of activities that include school work as well as social events. Being in school does not mean avoiding all non-academic relationships. However, you must be fully aware of your time commitments and make adjustments in these relationships. It would be an expensive lesson to fail or obtain low grades because you continued your non-academic relationships in a time consuming manner that adversely impacted your study efforts. Moderation and a commonsense approach should enable you to continue non-academic relationships without suffering from them. If you are a member of particular non-academic groups and associations, the same principles should apply. You can and should continue to maintain links but do it in moderation so that you still are able to accomplish your academic goals.

If you are working, then definitely include this in your commitments as it will take up your time. You have to compensate for working hours and make sure your course work does not suffer. As a student, your most precious commodity is time and the better you manage it, the more successful you will be. It is much easier to tackle academic work without having the burden of working. However, if you have to work, make sure that your school network is extra strong. If for any reason you miss a class, you can reach out to those in your network and find out what was covered as well as any other useful bits of information. It is safer to have several contacts to approach in such situations than to have only one contact person. What if your contact person also missed that same class? Or in some cases you will find out that not everyone in your network is focused and organized. As a result, when you approach such people for information about a class that you missed, they may not provide you with the most relevant material or information. This is not helpful to you in the least! Organize your study plan to ensure that you can keep up with the class. You may have to sacrifice more social activities to compensate for working.

## 2.10 Living On and Off Campus, which is Better?

The option you choose will depend on your individual circumstances. While many students may desire to stay on campus, the financial constraints may be too much to handle. Staying on campus provides a number of advantages to students. It allows for a conducive environment for studying. The library, classrooms, faculty and other students are all nearby. This enables a certain level of beneficial networking to take place.

Staying off campus means commuting and this takes a toll on ones' time. Off campus strategies for academic success include spending time at the library working on specific academic tasks such as completing assignments. Further, discussion groups could compel a student to spend more time on campus and gain the positive synergy of socializing and working with other students. Whether you are on or off campus, discipline, planning and organization are definitely keys to achieving academic success. Regardless of the option that you choose, stay focused and make adjustments to ensure that your academic endeavors are all in the right direction. Maintaining high grades should be your goal, regardless of whether you are on or off campus and you should work towards that.

## 2.11  Your Overall Academic Strategy; 4 Key Steps to Develop Your Study Plan

Step 1: List clearly all the activities that you have identified from the above. These include class schedules, assignments, projects, reports, presentations, exams, study group meetings, non-campus obligations and social activities. Note all deadlines and time frames for specific assignments/exams etc.

Step 2: It is helpful to utilize a color scheme in placing all these activities on your study plan. For example, one could use blue to indicate classes, green for exams, red to indicate assignments and yellow for private study sessions.

Step 3: On a weekly basis sum up how much time you spend on each course. Analyze your time allocation and determine whether you need to make any adjustments to compensate for extra work in some courses or a deficiency on your part in other courses.

Step 4: Make sure that your study plan includes adequate rest periods as well as social activities. Keep your schedule as realistic and achievable as possible.

## 2.12  Sample Study Plan

A sample study plan is provided in appendix 2. This type of plan can also be done on a monthly or a semester basis. A study plan can be designed in an excel spreadsheet. The most important thing about this plan is that it must contain all your time commitments. Create your own coding system to distinguish classes from study sessions etc. Every few weeks review your study plan to make sure it is effective. In other words, are you able to follow it? Does it provide you with adequate time to do all assignments? Identify aspects of your study plan that are not working and make adjustments to get better results. Make sure that the study plan is realistic and can be followed. If your study plan is accomplished with relative ease, it is a signal to beef it up to accomplish more.

## 2.13 Individual SWOT Analysis

Undertaking an Individual SWOT Analysis entails identifying your Strengths, Weaknesses, Opportunities and Threats. It is important to outline and be clear on the capabilities that you are working with. This will feed into the strategy that you will utilize to obtain the highest grades possible in your various courses. The SWOT Analysis should be mainly in relation to your academic efforts. The following can serve as a guideline to determining your Strengths, weaknesses, opportunities and threats:

Strengths: These would be particular skills and advantages that would enable you to succeed in academic terms. For example, good reading skills, excellent time management and quality writing skills would all fall under the category of strengths

Weaknesses: Under weaknesses one would include any factors that imply a deficiency in certain areas that weaken your overall academic capability; these would include for example poor reading skills or a math deficiency.

Opportunities: Any skills that could be utilized to enhance your overall academic performance can be placed under this category: for example, if you are good at working well with others and are also very organized, then these could be opportunities in that they can be utilized to enhance your academic performance.

Threats: Threats would include any factors that could adversely impact your academic performance; for example, having a large number of social commitments, working too many hours and not being able to focus while studying could all be considered as threats to your academic performance.

You can jot each of the points down in a simple bullet point format that you understand. For example, if you enjoy working well with numbers, then that would be put under strengths. If on the other hand you are not competent in using Microsoft Excel, then that would be a weakness and a possible threat. The reason it would be a possible threat is because you may be given assignments that require strong excel skills and your lack of competence in that area may mean spending more time to acquire the relevant skills before undertaking the task. This could then affect your overall academic effort. Critically review your SWOT Analysis to determine the possible impact on your academic progress. The aim of the SWOT Analysis is to use the results to make modifications in your study plan. For example, if math is a weakness, then your study plan should be structured in a manner that will show an increased effort to spend quality time improving your math skills. In other words, your study plan may have more time spent on studying math to make up for that particular deficiency identified in the SWOT Analysis.


"He that is good for making excuses is seldom good for anything else." Benjamin Franklin

# 3.0

# Ten Key Steps to Excellent Time Management

"He that rises late must trot all day."
Benjamin Franklin

Time is the key resource that all students have at their disposal. The difference between the academic performances of students can be linked directly to the manner in which each manages their time. Personal time management skills enable students to accomplish specific goals and tasks within a stipulated time period. The more successful you are in managing your time, the less stress that you will have while you are in school. In addition, you will feel increasingly confident as you continue to achieve and get things done and done well.

The following are Ten Time Management Steps for success:

Step 1: List and indicate clearly all tasks that have to be accomplished on a regular basis. Do not rely on your memory! There seems to be a certain power to writing things down.

Step 2: The order of items on your list should be reviewed to ensure that they are listed in order of importance; that is from the most important to the least important

Step 3: Assign specific times and dates to specific tasks; know when you are doing what

Step 4: A learning schedule or time table should reflect the level of priority of each task; that way you are always on top of the game and ahead of the curve.

Step 5: Do not schedule what you feel like doing, but what is necessary and relevant. Stay busy on the right things; those that will enable you to achieve your academic goals.

Step 6: Golden rule; stick to your plan. This is how you will succeed.

Step 7: Bad time management can be improved and changed; the first step is to look at the past and how you managed time and use the past to make specific changes to break away from those bad habits that denied you from accomplishing your goals and tasks etc.

Step 8: Make plans for each week or month, semester and calendar year

Step 9: As each item on the task list is accomplished it is important to check it off as completed. This has strong and positive motivational impact on the confidence level of the person accomplishing the tasks.

Step 10: Do not over commit yourself; make sure your tasks scheduled are achievable.

The time spent planning is a pain to many, but it pays off. It is a major reason why many do not plan; they do not want to waste time. However, by not planning, they do end up wasting time. Emergencies happen and you may fall off your schedule. The key to success is to minimize the amount of time that you fall off your schedule as well as to reorganize your schedule when such emergencies take place. Things will happen; your adjustment will help you to accomplish your goals.

Periodically, ask yourself the following questions:

- What have you accomplished this week/day?
- Were there any tasks that you failed to complete?
- If you answered yes to the previous question; why did you fail to complete those tasks?
- What steps can you take to ensure that you will have better results when trying to accomplish your tasks?

Effective time management will have a positive impact on your morale and this is important for doing well in school. Getting a grip on your academic responsibilities provides a peace of mind that can in turn have a positive impact on even your private life!

There are core challenges to implementing effective time management steps including the following:

- Being afraid of change
- Not being sure or certain about the future
- Allowing the misuse of time to create a negative pressure

To deal with these challenges, I suggest the following:

- Identify your specific fears and take note of each of them. Address these fears and ask yourself why you are afraid. Confront your fears squarely and address them.
- There is no shame in being unsure about the future. However, you can accomplish your goals if you clearly identify them and plan how to achieve each of them. In addition, researching and getting the right information can make you more prepared for the future.
- Even when you have mismanaged time, it is still possible to take a step back, reorganize and achieve one's goals. Do not wait until the last minute as this will create a unique challenge that may be overwhelming. When you fail to follow your time management plan, re-organize yourself and get back on track. Do everything possible to minimize the amount and length of time that is spent going off-track from your schedule.

By applying effective time management practices one will be able to:

- Increase overall efficiency; this means getting tasks completed well and on time
- Develop personal time management skills; this will overflow into other aspects of your life
- Approach tasks with less stress and more confidence

In conclusion, with effective time management you will be able to use your time in a much more balanced and results oriented manner. You will also be able to make time for the people and activities that you love. When you get to the end of a busy day, you'll feel a strong sense of accomplishment from everything that you actually accomplished!

In terms of time spent studying, remember that diminishing returns do set in eventually. It is important to diversify activities and utilize the time periods when one is most attentive to study. The importance of the activities should match the time.

It may be helpful to keep a daily journal that you can refer to and monitor your time management success. As mentioned earlier, there is a power in putting things on paper and monitoring your performance. You could even keep such a journal of notes on your cell phone.

"If you don't know where you are going, any road will get you there." Lewis Carroll (English Logician, Mathematician, Photographer and Novelist, especially remembered for Alice's Adventures in Wonderland. 1832-1898)

# 4.0

# Study Skills and Memory Retention

"I didn't fail the test; I just found 100 ways to do it wrong."
Benjamin Franklin

Successful studying is focused on retaining knowledge and being able to present it in the manner required. It is helpful to understand the overall learning process to ensure that you get the most out of the time that you spend studying. A key step in the process of retaining knowledge is the environment in which one attempts to do so. Each person has their own unique preferences. It is important to identify what type of environment works for you. A quiet place where you can focus without distractions and minimal temptations would enhance success. In addition, increased retention means utilizing less time to obtain more knowledge!

## 4.1 The Learning Process

Learning is about repetition. It is a process and the first stage starts with the lectures and listening. While most may forget about 80% of what they hear, this is a basis now to build on. The second stage is work on assignments, project work, research, textbook reviews and presentations. The final stage is the preparation for exams. The diagram below provides an outline of the three key stages of the learning process.

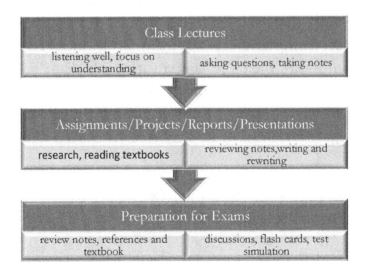

**The Three Key Stages of the Learning Process**

Each stage plays an important role in developing your knowledge base and in effect preparing you for the final stage; exams. For example, if you picked up 20% of the material in class, you could pick an additional 40% doing assignments etc. and the final 40% of the material preparing for exams. This spreads your study efforts in an effective manner. You are in effect increasing your chances of doing well in that particular course.

## 4.2 Stage 1: Lectures

Stage 1 of the learning process starts in the classroom; do not miss a single class if possible, because when you do, you can never get it back. Missing classes is tantamount to creating a hole in the ground that you have to fill at a later date when time is of essence. Those who attend classes regularly tend to be amongst the top performers in their class. Asking someone to brief you is the next best thing (other than recording the lectures). However, the best intentioned briefings will leave some important parts of the lecture out. Minimize the number of times that you have to backtrack to get information.

To obtain the most from lectures, it is important to ensure paying attention during class. There is the tendency for the mind to wander and at times some students leave a lecture and cannot remember a single thing that was mentioned! It takes a conscience effort to focus and follow the material being covered. The better a student understands what is discussed in class, the more efficient the whole learning cycle will be. To cement the knowledge gained from lectures it is important to ask questions. Make sure you get clarification on issues you are not clear about. Being too shy to ask questions will not work in your favor. Well-structured questions enable faculty to guide students towards the material that is most important. Do not be disturbed if you leave a class and know that there were some materials that slipped by you. Those materials should be your starting point when you begin to organize and undertake research using textbooks and other reference sources.

A key factor to note during lectures is that many faculty members provide tips, either consciously or unconsciously, these tips concern materials that should be well noted, possibly for examinations. The attentive students seem to grasp these tips and note them very well. In doing so they are able to focus on the most important points and their learning process is highly effective.

## 4.3 Stage 2: Notes Review/Assignments/ Projects/Reports/Presentations

The second stage in the learning process includes the review of notes, making references, revising textbooks, writing reports/assignments and making presentations. These activities will vary depending on the faculty teaching the course. Regardless, any combination of these activities is an opportunity to utilize the knowledge covered in class. This further cements the material in one's memory. If you spend quality time making notes, working on assignments, reviewing textbooks and conducting research, it will assist in remembering relevant information.

Note taking is an art. It is a major key to making life easier in the learning process. Your notes from classes are a first step. Whether one chooses to use shorthand or any other method of making notes, it is important to devise a system to obtain high quality notes. This will again ensure that you can identify exactly what to focus on when studying for examinations. It also assists with referencing materials out of the classroom. Making notes during class also performs an important function; the process compels you to take into account and follow the lecture fully. It is easier to follow a class and avoid losing concentration when you are writing notes. The last thing you want to do is sit in a two-hour class and listen only; your mind will begin to wander. In addition, you will leave the class empty handed. You still may have to prepare those notes from a textbook later on, which may be time consuming and more difficult.

Your notes from class may not be perfect and you may have to spend time to enhance them. Review your lecture notes with the objective of enhancing them by adding research references and material from the course textbook. Remember that well prepared notes mean reading the textbook less. This becomes especially important as one approaches exams and time is of essence. For example, if the key textbook for the course contains 1,000 pages, it can be blended with your notes to create a 100-page document. Studying 100 pages of notes days and weeks before an exam gives one a better chance of remembering key points as opposed to studying 1,000 pages of a textbook! Make sure that you work this reality to your advantage. It is advisable to review notes immediately after lectures so as not to lose key points and concepts. When possible, borrow notes from others to make sure you captured the most important points. This also enables you to fill any potholes (areas you simply could not follow during the lecture) that you may have in your notes. These days many professors provide slides of their presentations. These slides should be printed prior to the lecture and used as the basis for writing notes in class. The slides allow for better organization of materials and minimize confusion about what has and has not been covered in class. Using the slides also minimizes potholes and the time and effort required to record notes as the skeleton is already provided.

It is very important to take note of articles and other reference materials either given out to the class by the professor or mentioned during the class. This will save time in referencing materials and allow you to focus on the relevant materials. The key is to avoid being lazy and letting such valuable information slip away. It may be more expensive in terms of your time to go back and find these references from others.

In this era of computers and the internet; all students have a unique advantage. Whether at home or in the library there is no shortage of computers for students to use. Using search engines like Google can assist a student to beef up notes, reference key materials and add strong points that can make the difference between an A grade and a B or C grade. In making notes as well as summaries, it is possible to use a color scheme such as red, gold and green to signify the level of importance of different topics and points. This sharpens the focus on specific materials that must be retained for sure in preparing for an exam.

## 4.4  Stage 3: Preparation for Examinations

The essence of the various study methods is to retain knowledge that you can easily recall. The better you get at doing this the better your test performances. Putting in quality work on stages 1 and 2 will make stage 3 easier. There are many types of study methods and successful students utilize a vast array and combination of these methods. Choosing a study method should be like selecting food from a menu in a restaurant. One has to survey the different study methods and pick the ones that seem most appropriate. If a particular method does not work for you, drop it and focus on the ones that do work. Never choose a method because it works for others, chose it because it works for you!

## 4.5  Study Methods

A key study method that can provide success in the exam preparation process is the PQRST method. It provides structure and by following the steps consistently, you will recognize a continuous improvement in your knowledge base with time.

The key element of this method is prioritizing the information required to pass an exam. This method provides ample room for modification to suit each student. PQRST stands for **P**review, **Q**uestion, **R**ead, **S**ummarize and **T**est.

> **Preview:** At this stage simply review the topic to be learnt by glossing over the key headings and points especially as indicated in the course outline.

> **Question:** Write down a list of questions about each topic and sub topic after reviewing the material thoroughly.

> **Read:** Use the questions (you can also use assignments and other questions found within the course textbook) as a guide to review all your notes as well as the

reference materials and the textbook for the course. Your aim is to make sure that you can answer all the questions that you have compiled.

**Summarize:** At this stage your job is to summarize the various topics in a manner that is totally your own. It is at this stage that you can utilize written notes; an array of diagram types, mnemonics or even voice recordings. Choose the methods that you are most comfortable with.

**Test:** Finally, the test stage is where you go back to the questions and try to answer the most important ones (based on emphasis in class, course outlines assignments etc.) in as detailed a manner as possible. To gain from this stage it is better to attempt answering the questions from memory. After answering the questions, you can then refer to reference materials and check to determine how well the questions were answered. Going through this process as many times as possible is a strong way of retaining relevant material for an exam. It is important to narrow down the questions to be answered and focus on those most relevant for the exam as the 'D' day approaches. This process allows you to recognize important topics that one is not prepared for and allows you to then address this situation.

## 4.6 Mnemonics

A key element in the PQRST method is the use of mnemonics. This is a very helpful way of retaining specific points in an organized manner. For example, an economics student may be trying to remember the factors that influence the demand for a product (the determinants of demand) apart from price. These would include taste, number of buyers, income of the consumer, prices of other goods and consumer expectations. The next stage is to create an acronym utilizing the first letter of each key point (phrase or word). For example, T for taste, N for number of buyers, I for income, P for prices of other goods and E for expectations. The next stage is to put the letters together to form a word such as T.N.I.P.E. By remembering T.N.I.P.E. the student recalls the factors that cause demand to change or the determinants of demand.

It is important to start using this method at latter stages of the semester so that the key words actually mean something to you and by remembering the key words you then recall the related explanations. Other than that one is memorizing for memorizing sake, which is not helpful under exam conditions.

## 4.7 Flash Cards (Index Cards):

Flash cards are an effective revision tool. It is ideal to develop them during revision periods. By this time most students are aware of the exact materials that they have to remember. In addition, cards allow you to focus on the most essential points. That is why it is ideal to develop Flash cards after the material has been studied and understood to a large extent. The focus is now remembering or retaining specific sets of knowledge. The acronyms developed earlier can all be placed on the cards. These cards can then be revised almost anywhere! When developing Flash Cards; be sure to focus especially on key points that you are having problems remembering. In some cases, Flash Cards may be available for some courses. These tend to be well organized. When possible, it is highly recommended that you obtain access to these cards. While some of the available flash cards may be only obtained by purchasing them, it could prove to be a very worthy investment. Acquiring pre-designed flash cards could save time in designing your own. After all, time is the most precious commodity for every student!

In conclusion, avoid rote learning as much as possible. Many studies indicate that it is not effective in the long run at the college and university level. It however, may be necessary for some courses such as languages. Make sure to review your materials as often as possible.

"The heights by great men reached and kept were not attained by sudden flight, but they, while their companions slept, were toiling upward in the night." Henry Wadsworth Longfellow

# 5.0

# Handling Math Successfully

"Neglect of mathematics works injury to all knowledge, since he who is ignorant of it cannot know the other sciences or the things of the world."
Roger Bacon

There are many students who have had challenges with math and math related courses. This trend is an on-going battle and the fact is, sooner or later the problem has to be faced head on. Why, because the requirements for many courses include passing varying levels of math, algebra and statistics. The history of this problem possibly stems from not learning the fundamentals properly. Spending little time practicing is also a contributory factor for many students facing math challenges. Math is like layers of material that support each other. Multiplication and division are a basis for further sub-topics. If you are weak in multiplication, then it follows that you will have problems dealing with topics that rely on multiplication as a layer or a basis.

**Fractions Statement**

The shocking reality and good news is that, when tackled properly, math can be one of the subjects that students stand a chance to score the highest possible grades in!

How can we deal with the math challenge? First of all, it is important to identify exactly what layers of knowledge (math) are missing for each student. Your missing layers may be different from another student. It is these missing layers of knowledge that make math so difficult for some. Without a strong foundation in earlier layers/materials, it is difficult to build and add more knowledge.

## 5.1  Ten Steps to Handling Math

Step 1: Find out your true math level. Identify a book or several math books that cover a range of key topics that you have been taught to this point. Then take a sample of questions and attempt them.

Step 2: Mark your answers and use the results to list all the topics that you did not do well in.

Step 3: Prepare a study plan to review and practice the identified topics that you are weak in.

Step 4: If there are other challenges that you face in general, such as a lack of interest, etc. then list those under other challenges. Determine how to deal with these identified challenges. Discuss the other challenges with teachers and other students and find out how to deal with these issues. Listen carefully to their ideas and pick the ones that work for you.

Step 5; Make sure that your study plan is realistic in terms of adequate time to review and practice each topic on your list. Do not be intimidated if you have a large number of topics to cover! Be consistent in your review and you will make remarkable progress improving your math IQ (Intelligence Quotient).

Step 6: Work consistently to begin filling in the missing layers. For example, your study plan could have a strategy of devoting one hour every single day to working on math problems. Make sure you choose easy to understand books and workbooks with numerous questions as well as answers.

Step 7: After trying a number of questions for each topic, review the answers and identify those that you got wrong. Go through the wrong answers carefully to identify exactly why you got them wrong. It is important to go through the same questions you got wrong as many times as necessary until you have been able to understand the process of working through the questions to the right answer.

Step 8: List again all the topics/sub-topics that are still troubling you. Go through practice questions and review guidelines for answering these questions carefully.

Step 9: Bring in tutors when you have spent time making several efforts on your own to resolve problems. If you do use a tutor, make sure to note the exact process that is used to eventually solve the problem and practice until you get all those types of problems correct. Remember, you are trying to improve your math skills and the more work that you do on your own the higher your math skill level rises. Note that it is very important to start the process by working on your own before bringing in tutors. This allows you to start identifying specific areas of challenge that you definitely need help on.

Step 10: Develop a little book where you keep track of all formulae, steps and strategies. Review this and practice as often as you can until these concepts and formulae are part of your mental machinery. Give your problems a final do-over and see whether there are any problems that are still beating you. If there are, then this would be the ideal stage to bring in outside help. Note carefully the methods your tutor uses and try them on your own using several different problems until you are comfortable with them.

The previous steps are designed to fill in the missing layers of math knowledge that you may have as well as provide a strong basis to now go on to add more math knowledge in an effective manner. After going through the above exercise, your math capabilities will definitely see an improvement. You will no longer have to comment that you are deficient in math! Your confidence in yourself will be boosted and you will be able to face academic challenges with a greater level of courage.

## 5.2 The Right Way to Use Tutoring Services

To develop your math level, it is important that you minimize the use of tutors as much as possible. While this may seem hard initially, it will assist you to strengthen your math skills. Your capacity to independently solve math problems will rise as you make effort to strengthen your math skills. However, do not fall into the pattern of avoiding tutoring to look cool or to hide the fact that you need help. If you need assistance, by all means go out and get it! Everyone is different and needing assistance does not in any way make you inferior to your classmates. It would be painful to realize that had you gone for tutoring you could have passed all your courses and saved yourself time and money doing courses over again. Excessive tutoring on the other hand is like a bad short cut and in effect:

- Minimizes the opportunities you can have to tackle the problem that is yours and not the tutors
- It also creates a level of dependency amongst many students
- In addition, the tutors assist you on current problems without tackling the real issue at stake, the topics and sub-topics that are rendering you ineffective in tackling current problems.

The ten key steps highlighted above will help you to improve your math skills. The major point is that practice makes perfect. Remember that the weaker you are in math, or the more topics you do not understand, then the more time you should put aside to improve your math skills. The continuous testing and reviewing will pay off in terms of your improved individual performance. When you start seeing improved performance on exams etc., remember what got you to that stage; practice! If you want to continue improving or maintaining your math capability (you should be aiming for the former!), then you will have to keep on practicing. Make sure you vary the problems you try and gradually build up from easy ones to difficult ones. Challenge yourself each time to continue improving your level of understanding of math concepts and processes.

Do not despair when certain problems prove difficult. Those are the math muscle building opportunities and you should welcome those opportunities with confidence, telling yourself, "I can do this!"

Many schools have various math challenge exams that students are allowed to take to determine their true math level. Make sure you are well prepared before taking any of such exams. Otherwise you could confuse yourself in terms of identifying the actual topics that are giving you problems. These exams are very helpful in determining the topics that you are weak in. Do not underestimate any of the topics and continue to practice until you are clearly becoming more proficient in each topic.

## 5.3  Internet Sources of Math Support

With internet access, you can use blogs and work with others to develop your math aptitude. In addition, there are a number of websites that provide support and strategies. You can use online sources to find math drills and practice math tests. Computers can be very helpful in developing math capacity. Use them to your advantage.

The following website is meant for high school and college students as well as adult learners and covers a wide range of topics from algebra to trigonometry:

http://www.sosmath.com/

You can also obtain online tutoring from the following sources:

http://www.tutorvista.com/bow/improve-math-skills
http://mathforum.org/dr/math/faq/faq.why.math.html

Feel free to research for other sources of assistance on-line. Check them thoroughly to make sure that the site has the relevant material to enable you to upgrade your math skills.

It could be helpful to find course outlines for lower math levels and use these to identify topics to review. Look for older math books that you have used in the past to also assist in identifying topics to review. All these help in focusing on the topics that you need to build up on.

By improving your math skills, you may actually be building your confidence and ability to approach other courses with greater success. This is because practicing math is an excellent brain exercise.

"It is not enough to have a good mind. The main thing is to use it well" Rene Descartes

# 6.0

# Reading Skills and Speed Reading

"If a man empties his purse into his head, no one can take it from him."
Benjamin Franklin

The Webster dictionary defines Speed reading as "a method of reading rapidly by skimming". Other definitions assert that it is a collection of reading methods focused on increasing rates of reading while maintaining the level of comprehension. Strong reading skills will have a positive impact on your academic progress; the reverse is also true. Research has shown that speed reading skills are not grasped by everyone who tries to learn them. However, you will not know unless you try. Even if you do not become an avid speed reader, many of the steps are such that it will help you to improve your overall comprehension skills. This is important for any course. Many avid readers have unconsciously developed speed reading skills because of the large volume of material they read regularly.

What are the benefits of effective speed reading?

- If you read regularly and make a conscience effort to develop your reading skill it will have a positive impact on your academic performance.
- It will reduce the amount of time you need to read through materials
- It will enhance your ability to recognize important points and key issues in your readings.
- It is also an important skill on the job; employer surveys indicate that 63% of employers ranked reading comprehension as very important.

Before trying to speed read, it is important to be a basically good reader. Otherwise you are going a step too quickly and could end up losing your comprehension rate. If you are not a strong reader, then try these steps to strengthen your reading skills:

**Library books**

## 6.1 General Steps to Improve Reading Skills:

Step 1: Develop a plan to read books of your preference on a daily basis.

Step 2: Monitor how long it takes you to read a book.

Step 3: After reading each book, prepare a list of basic questions; who, what, where, when, how etc. and answer them without help from the book.

Step 4: Go back to the book and check your performance.

Step 5: Continue to do this with each new book until you realize that your score and performance is consistent; in other words, you have attained a high level of comprehension.

Step 6: Compare how long it takes you now to read a book. The time should have reduced.

The key method to develop speed reading focuses around actually reading! That is the first step. There is no substitute for this. It is only by reading that you can gauge your initial speed, then by implementing the techniques of speed reading you can compare the before and after to assess the extent to which your speed has increased. Basically, you do not need to be the fastest reader in the world. Your aim is to get the key points from material that you read as quickly as possible.

There are a number of courses geared towards training people on speed reading. These are at times costly and take up a lot of time. If you can find a way to utilize them, do so. However, the following is a simplified 10 step approach that captures the most important aspects of speed reading. The following information will get you started in a simple and effective manner.

## 6.2 Ten Key Steps to Speed Reading:

Step 1: Choose a quiet and peaceful environment; Make all efforts to read without any distractions at all. If you have distractions, you give your brain more work to do in moving the distractions to the background. That brain work (noise cancellation) reduces your ability to comprehend at a greater rate. Many suggest reading early in the day when the brain is fresh.

Step 2: Start your speed reading exercise using articles; scan them;

Step 3: Then read just the first sentence of each paragraph initially, as the first sentence usually is a summary of the whole paragraph

Step 4: Now read the whole article, but make an intentional effort to read through it quicker than the first time. The reason for this is that when reading we do not realize that our eyes are quick. We tend to slow our eyes down! So speed it up and go through the whole document. In effect we are all quicker readers, but do not realize it!

Step 5: The next step is to develop the skill of recognizing phrases and words that you can skip without losing the trend of the discussion. These are the general words and terms one finds in most materials. Let your mind focus on new and important words and points. This will assist you to increase your speed of reading.

Step 6: Do not expect to understand everything that you read the first time that you read it! With each reading your mind will begin to identify and focus on the important terms and points being discussed. That is exactly what you are trying to develop, the ability to determine the key points. Trying to understand everything the first time you read it is like going from 0 – 100 miles in seconds. It is unnatural and will not happen! Consider that when you read a book the second or third time, you get a different level of appreciation for it!

Step 7: As you continue reading your mind will give you a signal when it needs a break. Take a break! Many try to ignore this and continue reading. They are able to read but at diminishing returns in terms of comprehension. Refreshing and going back ensures that your efficiency is high each time you read.

Step 8: Practice makes perfect. The above steps are the fundamental steps in speed reading. The next step is to practice using different materials. It helps to time yourself initially so that you can compare over time how much your speed has improved. As you continue to practice you will develop your own rhythm for ignoring certain words etc. while still grasping the meaning of what you are reading. That is what you are looking for. Practice is the most important element of reading fast. Without doing this regularly, it will be hard for your speed to increase in a meaningful manner.

Step 9: Test by asking yourself questions about the article to make sure you were able to comprehend the most important points. Do this with each new article that you read.

Step 10: Graduate from articles to books using all of the steps above. You can start with books right away, however simple steps at times bring the most effective results.

Before graduating from speed reading articles to your first book, ask yourself the following questions:

- Why are you about to read the book, what are you trying to get out of the book?
- From the cover, title, table of contents, headings, sub headings, introduction or preface and back page, can you determine the message the author is trying to get across?

The following tips will be helpful when you begin reading books:

- Focus on the message in each chapter
- The last paragraph of each chapter contains the main essence of the chapter and is worth reading twice
- Always preview the chapter before you settle down to read it; you are previewing to get the general message
- Look out for the key points as well as important dates, places etc.

A number of groups have researched and identified that most online speed reading courses are frauds and do not benefit customers who sign up. Be careful in selecting speed reading programs.

## 6.3  Online Resources

There are a number of free speed reading resources online that can assist you to enhance your reading skills. The following suggested websites are amongst such free resources.

http://www.readingsoft.com/

This site provides speed reading tests online. The site also provides a grading system to determine the level of reading capability.

http://www.freereadingtest.com/

This is another site that provides free reading tests to determine one's reading level.

It is advisable to search and select the resources that work best for you. The key is to utilize the existing resources to improve upon your reading speed and comprehension. These skills will always be helpful throughout your academic journey.

"Tell me and I forget. Teach me and I remember. Involve me and I learn." Benjamin Franklin

# 7.0

# Writing Quality Papers

"Hide not your talents. They for use were made. What's a sundial in the shade?"
Benjamin Franklin

This chapter is focused on providing a simple strategy for writing quality business and project reports. The ultimate goal of writing a report is preparing one that effectively expresses the thoughts of the author. In addition, the report should be understood by the intended recipient(s). If you are given specific guidelines as well, then these must be covered. All of this requires effort, logic and consistency in approach. As with many things in life, you will realize that the more you practice and actually write reports, the better you will become at it. Take note that you will improve at a faster pace if your writing efforts are always well organized, focused and consistent in approach. This chapter is about assisting you to develop that consistent and effective writing approach. Following are 5 key steps that will ensure that your reports are the best they can be.

## 7.1 The Five Key Steps to Writing a Quality Research Paper:

Step 1: Identify clearly the topic of the report and prepare a list of various sub-topics and areas to research. Get started on the right foot by making sure you are very clear on the focus of the report. Write down the focus of your report in addition to the topics to research. While this may sound very simple, it is the most basic starting point. Your adherence to this step properly will mean that you will be able to get started on the right foot. You need to understand clearly exactly what you are supposed to be writing about. Many writers who fail to write properly are guilty of not recognizing clearly the topic and sub topics that they are to write on.

Step 2: Prepare an Outline. Based on the preliminary understanding and activities in step 1, develop a basic outline for your report. The outline should include the following amongst others:

a. Executive Summary
b. Introduction
c. Main Body/Key points

    d.  Conclusion

    e.  Bibliography

If you have an outline from the beginning of your writing effort this means that you have a game plan. You know exactly what you are trying to accomplish and in what order. Be sure to make modifications in your outline to match what you recognize as the key areas of importance based on the research topic/subtopics.

Step 3: Research the topic and sub-topics. Be thorough and utilize as many legitimate sources of information as possible. Note the sources of all your information. Your task is to accumulate as much reference material as possible. The sources of information should include the library, internet websites, journals, magazines, newspapers etc. Contact the librarian and find out whether they might be able to assist you in identifying specific sources of information on your topic. Quality information is the most important basis for writing a quality report. Many reports fall short of the mark because the writer failed to adequately research the topic. This is often due to laziness and a desire to save time. It does take time to research properly and you must start writing your report as early as possible to enable you to properly research the topic. An important point that you should note is that in many cases the Instructor is knowledgeable about the topic. As a result, any lazy efforts with minimal research will be recognized by your professor. This will not earn you any goodwill or a high grade!

Be sure to develop a system or format for organizing your research findings. If your research material is scattered and disorganized, it makes it difficult for you to review and utilize the material properly. You can choose for example to read articles, books and other publications and summarize them into a notebook. Be sure to note the sources of the materials in your notebook. Another option may be to make copies of specific pages and sections of the materials you read. However, this still leaves you with the task of sifting through all the pages to identify relevant material. If you do choose to make copies of pages, then you can go through them at a later date and color code the most important sections that you intend to utilize. You can also add comments to the pages to assist you in recognizing the sections that you intend to utilize and the manner in which you want to utilize those sections.

Step 4: Review all the information you have obtained and look out for the most relevant materials. This stage allows you to become even more familiar with the materials that you have gathered. If upon going through the material you realize that certain sections are not really relevant, please remove them from your research materials. Do not force yourself to utilize material simply because you spent time copying or summarizing them. If it is not relevant, then leave it out! By becoming familiar with the material you will find it much easier to write about the material and most importantly, put points into your own words. This point cannot be explained enough. Ultimately, your report should reflect your own words. The last thing that you want is to be accused of plagiarism. These days there are an array of software that can easily detect plagiarism. Avoid plagiarism at all costs.

Step 5: Organize the information according to its usefulness and area of concentration, for example charts, data and other exhibits can be put together. This will make it easy to refer and utilize the materials you have obtained on the topic. For example, all material related to your main body should be categorized as such. This will make it much easier for you to use the material as you begin to write your paper.

Step 6: Based on all the above, you may review your outline to ensure that it can capture the most relevant information that you have obtained. Only make absolutely necessary changes that you think will enhance the overall paper. Remember, you developed an outline to capture the essence of the topic of research and it should be consistent with your research and the information that you have gathered.

Step 7: Write your first draft. Follow your outline and write out the first draft of your report. Ensure that you include the most important points. This is where your organized research material will prove most helpful. By constantly referring to your research material you will have credible information to base your research upon. In addition, you will be able to recognize which sections should contain which information. Keep the English simple and from the very first draft make continuous effort to ensure that your grammar is accurate and proper. Where relevant be sure to use appropriate terms and concepts that will go a long way towards convincing any reader that you have a command over the subject matter by virtue of your research efforts. Remember, you are trying to make a point with your paper. The point being that you researched effectively, understood the material and as a result are able to write effectively on the topic. Always keep in mind the fact that your professors are able to read your report and determine your level of effort and understanding of the material.

Step 8: Review your draft report. It is almost impossible to prepare a draft report that will be your best possible output. Read through your draft report and ask yourself a series of questions. For example, does the report contain all the key points that you identified? Did you explain all your points properly? In terms of order, did you follow the outline? Were you able to include relevant statistics and charts that would strengthen your report? Did you make proper reference to those graphs and tables? Does your report contain reference to specific sources of information that you utilized? Did you include the appropriate terms and concepts? All these questions could lead you to recognizing specific areas for improvement. It may be helpful to jot your comments and recognized changes onto your draft report at the relevant sections.

Based upon your various comments after reading the draft report, you are then ready to rewrite the report by making all the changes that you identified. When you have finished making all corrections and changes, undertake a spell check. One important point to note at this stage is that during your review you may realize that there are certain points that you found inadequate because your research on those points was too shallow. If that is the case, go back and research those points to obtain adequate material. You should recognize that if you found the material shallow, then the chances are high that your instructor will find it shallow as well. This process should be repeated until your report is complete. You will know when the report is complete because at that stage you do not see any changes (apart from minor ones) to make that would improve it. Make sure you have included the relevant charts, graphs, tables, exhibits and quotations. Make sure that your report follows the outline that you prepared. Stay on track to avoid deviating. Look for the following when you are reviewing your report:

- Consistency in approach: the whole paper should have a consistency in terms of your writing focus.
- Effectiveness in making the relevant points: In undertaking your paper there were clear objectives that you set out to achieve and it is important that you make sure you achieve these objectives. Your points should be clear and easy to understand.
- Grammatical errors: It sounds so mundane, yet too often students submit papers without undertaking a thorough review. The result; avoidable grammatical errors that could have been removed with a simple spell check! Running spell check several times will help to remove as many errors as possible. Any such errors that are in your paper indicate to the reader (your instructor) that little time was spent on basic editing of the paper. That kind of impression will not gain you any positive goodwill when your paper is being graded.

- Accuracy of data, dates, quotes and charts etc.: Double check all quotes, data etc. and make sure of their accuracy. Errors in these areas also give a very bad impression as quality editing would have afforded you an opportunity to identify them and take action.

- Smoothness of the report; how the report reads overall: Ask yourself whether the report has a good flow and provides all the relevant answers? Does it reflect the overall topic and sub-topics? Is the order of material appropriate or is there the need to reorder some of the paragraphs?

- Make sure all exhibits included in the report are properly labeled and actually referred to in emphasizing specific points. All too often, exhibits are included in a report without the author making appropriate reference to them. This begs the question as to why these exhibits were included if they were not being used to make specific points. Ensure that every exhibit is properly referenced and discussed. In fact, before putting in any exhibits ensure that you understand exactly the point that each one is making. Your exhibits should be included in your report to support points and enrich your paper and not to make your final report bulky.

- Have someone else go through your report. When you feel you are finished, let a new set of eyes review the report and give comments to improve it. More often than not, another person reading your report can give you a fresh perspective with suggestions that could help improve your paper. Use your discretion when considering comments from others. You do not have to implement every single comment but rather those that clearly make sense to you and would definitely improve the quality of the paper.

- The review process should be done as many times as possible before the report is due. Even the best writers insist that this stage is what leads to the best writing! Do not skimp on reviewing your paper. In many cases it is at this stage that the report really becomes a quality paper as each edit leads to improvements in the paper. Without a thorough review being undertaken, there are often tell-tale signs that the author did not spend much time improving the paper. This will not encourage your instructor to give you the best grade possible.

After completing the above steps you are now ready to prepare your bibliography. This list should include all reference materials that you utilized in preparing the report. It is your responsibility to honestly and accurately indicate all sources of information for your report. Internet websites that were utilized should all be included. Sources of quotations should be specifically referred to. A check online will provide ample guides concerning how to use quotation as well as how to prepare bibliographies.

The following are sites that can assist in preparing a bibliography:

## Easybib

This site assists with writing a bibliography. In addition, there is a checker to ensure that one does not plagiarize. The site also allows for a grammar check. It covers various formats including MLA, APA and the Chicago bibliography formats. While the basic edition is free, the more advanced edition is $9.95 per month.

## CitationMachine

Very similar to Easybib, this site also provides assistance with writing a bibliography as well as checking spelling and grammar in a report. The site has a basic edition that is free and a paid edition with advanced and varied options. The paid edition is also $9.95 per month.

There are a number of things that can make your paper stand out compared to others. The vocabulary used in the paper should be relevant to the topic. In addition, new terms and concepts should be used properly. Do not hesitate to use a dictionary to ensure that you are using new vocabulary in the proper manner.

Varying your first sentence of each paragraph will keep your paper fresh and interesting. When a paper is boring it does not give the instructor much of a reason to give it a high grade. However, in many cases, it is important to keep your writing simple and effective in terms of getting your message across. You will have higher grades by writing clear and concise papers than complicated ones that are hard to understand. Remember, if any part of your paper does not make sense to you, then do not expect it to make sense to others who read it.

Writing skills improve with regular practice. It is as simple as that. If you write infrequently, it is difficult to develop a rhythm and style of your own. Your writing skills will not improve if you do not write and write often! However, by writing consistently using the suggested format, you will realize that with time you will be able to identify your own steps, short cuts and methods of writing effectively. No matter the methods you choose, remember, there is no alternative for reviewing and rewriting. Even the best writers in history noted that revision is an important part of the writing process. Perhaps it can be said that it is the art of revision and editing that distinguishes good writers from great writers and average writers from good writers! Remember, your grades will depend on quality writing and the earlier you develop your writing skills the better.

At the end of the day your report should be a smooth, well organized write up that is yours. In other words, you should end up with a report that you fully wrote and one that in no way can be confused with someone else's work. Your report should not include sections that are copied from other sources word for word. Do not commit this cardinal offense of plagiarism. If for any reason you find the need to use someone else's words, then be sure to use quotation marks and note clearly the source of those words. As mentioned earlier, in this modern era, there are a variety of software that can easily tell your professor exactly where certain phrases or sentences came from. In fact, simply putting a sentence in Google can tell someone where certain words were picked from! It is highly important that you write your own paper and develop your own style. That way you will become a confident and able writer. As you continue to write reports using the suggested steps in this chapter you will realize that your writing skills will continue to improve. You will confidently be able to develop your reports and write them with effectiveness. In addition, anyone who reads your report will appreciate the effort that went into it as well as your effectiveness as a writer. That is exactly what you are trying to accomplish! Remember that quality reports do not mean fancy English! Keep it simple, organized and well structured so that anyone who reads it will be able to understand the report and the points that you were trying to make. Most important of all, practice and remember that the more you write, the better that you will become at it!

"Without continual growth and progress, such words as improvement, achievement, and success have no meaning." Benjamin Franklin

# 8.0

# Making Great Presentations

"Be a yardstick of quality. Some people aren't used to an
environment where excellence is expected."
Steve Jobs

These days most courses require students to undertake presentations on various subjects. Presentation skills have become even more relevant as technology for presenting such as Microsoft PowerPoint; video clips etc. continue to increase. Indeed, it is rare these days to go to a presentation and not see Microsoft PowerPoint being utilized. The culture of presentations is prevalent in many working environments. Consequently, by honing your skills in school, you may be rewarded with good grades as well as having a strong presentation capability in the work environment! As a future manager/leader, having excellent presentation skills will definitely be an asset to you during your career. Do not waste the opportunities that you get to present in school. Experience is the best teacher and it would be preferable that you make mistakes in school while honing your presentation skills than on the job when mistakes could be very costly to your career.

Following is an easy to use guide for how to develop a great presentation as well as how to present effectively.

## 8.1 Creating the Presentation

Step 1: Identify and understand clearly the purpose (or subject matter) of the presentation: One of the most common sources of confusion when it comes to making presentations, is the fact that the presenter did not clearly understand the exact reason for making the presentation. Do not leave room for any ambiguity when it comes to the topic of the presentation. That way all your hard work will not go in vain and your audience will not be confused and dissatisfied that your presentation differs from their expectations.

Step 2: Know your audience and their characteristics (keep this in mind as you develop your presentation to ensure that your material is consistent with your audience): In many cases you should have a decent idea about the type of people that will be listening to your presentation. If you are presenting a paper to parents concerning the Impact of the 2008 economic crisis on college students, then you might analyze your audience as follows:

Statement of Purpose: This presentation is being made to depict the impact of the 2008 economic crisis on college students
Audience Profile:

- Audience: The audience shall consist of parents of college students
- Age range: 35 – 60 years
- Education: mixed; in other words, high school/GED, College, Postgraduate etc.
- Sex: 65% females 35% males
- Economic background: lower and middle level

The above profile clearly gives you an indication of the audience that you will be presenting to. This should be done before you begin your research and will be of assistance as you put your presentation together. For example, from the profile above, you are definitely going to be speaking with a mature audience. This means your material should be relevant and on point with accurate facts and figures (including quoting sources). The mixed education level means that your material should be well understood by all regardless of their education level. In other words, all your points and materials would be most understood if kept simple and straight to the point.

Step 3: Do your research thoroughly; using the internet etc.: Now that you are clear on your topic as well as your audience, it is time to undertake the core research for your presentation. This is an important aspect of your preparation process. Be sure to make adequate time to research your topic. There are no short cuts available when it comes to undertaking adequate research for your presentation. Know that everyone in your audience will have some knowledge of the topic and your inability to research properly will be exposed! Do not allow this to happen. There are many sources of information and the more sources that you use the better.

When researching your presentation topic take particular note of the following:

- List specifically the information you are seeking: this will make it easier to identify/find
- Use this list as a guide in collecting information for your presentation: as simple as this sounds it serves as a check to ensure you stay on point in terms of finding relevant information. It also allows you to keep track of information that you have yet to gather or obtain material on.

- Internet – Google, organizational websites, government websites, and corporate websites: the online sources of information continue to increase on a daily basis. Be sure to thoroughly check the relevant sources of information. For example, if you are making a presentation on unemployment, then you should be checking for the Government website that regularly provides statistics on this.

- Try a variation of phrases to get different types of information: sometimes when searching for information online initial searches may not provide you with much in terms of relevant material. This may not be because such information does not exist but rather may require a different type of phrasing of words or reordering of words. Try also changing the terms to see whether the search results you get are different and more helpful.

- The library has access to websites you normally have to pay for: Most schools have databases that they subscribe to for the benefit of faculty and students. It is important to tap into such sources of information for your research. Your librarian would know which databases are available for specific topics. Quality information from reliable sources will help you to develop a presentation that is clearly well researched and professional. That is exactly the impression you want to create for your audience!

- Identify and chat with experts on your topic: More often than not we forget that speaking with experts on any particular topic can be a very enriching experience. There are knowledge experts on a variety of topics out there. It only takes identifying and approaching them for assistance and information. Be sure to have questions ready for such experts. For example, a presentation on Barnes and Noble may be enriched by visiting the company and speaking with a manager in the relevant department who has worked in that field for a decent period of time. That person may have information that would assist you to understand the topic clearly. You can reference such an interview in your presentation and it definitely shows that you undertook thorough research on the topic.

- Use various books, magazines, journals, newspapers etc.: In terms of using a variety of sources of information, we should not forget the more common ones such as books, journals, periodicals, magazines and newspapers. As with all your other sources of information, be sure to take note of exactly where the information is coming from so that you can include it in your bibliography. While a bibliography may not be mandatory for a presentation, go ahead and put one together anyway. It serves to provide you with a backdrop should you need to undertake further research. In addition, any questions related to certain aspects of your presentation can be supported with your bibliography. Finally, a detailed bibliography shows the serious research that you put into the presentation and this is a plus for you!

- Collect data that can strengthen your points: As you continue to research, remember that facts and figures are always strong in helping you to make relevant points. Be sure to organize any data you obtain properly. Remember though that you are interested in relevant data and not just data for the sake of data. Always state or note the sources of your data. They should be verifiable and you should make all efforts to let that information be known.

- Put the data into friendly formats such as spreadsheets, charts and diagrams: When possible, modify the data into charts and diagrams to make it easy for your audience to understand the point you are trying to make. For example, if you are presenting on the financial performance of Apple for the past 10 year, a line chart showing the net profits might be the best way to go. A line chart that reveals a continuous upward increase in profits does not require much explanation. In addition, it is irrefutable as all can see the line moving on a positive upward slope with time. The charts do not have to be complex at all. They should simply use the data gathered to help you tell a story/make specific points. Having several charts through-out your presentation can make it very effective and easily understood.

- Verify the sources of your data and ensure that there is reliability and consistency: It pays to double check all the data in your presentation. The last thing you want is for someone to point out that certain data you utilized may be inaccurate! A question mark on one data point may lead your audience to question all your data points!

- Create an outline for your presentation; make sure that it has a logical sequence: By creating a logical and consistent outline, you make your work easy. Your task would then be to follow the outline and fill in the relevant material. A consistent outline also makes it easy for your audience to follow and understand your presentation. That should be a major focus for you; ensuring that your audience is able to easily comprehend the presentation that you have put together. Similar to writing a report, your presentation structure should include the following;
  Beginning - what you are trying to accomplish
  Key Points – the points to note/discuss/expatiate on
  Conclusion – what you have accomplished

## 8.2  Key Points to Note when Developing Your Presentation:

Keep it simple: When organizing your presentation, it is always best to keep it straightforward. This increases the probability that everyone will understand the points you are trying to make. The last thing you want to do is to confuse your audience. Your aim is to provide your audience with information that will let them leave knowing for sure that they gained something from your presentation.

Keep it professional: Throughout your preparation and research ensure that the material gathered and the manner in which you utilize the material is both economical and professional.

Keep it interesting: Simply putting loads of facts together may bore your audience. Determine the manner in which you will organize your material so that it remains not only informative but interesting.

Make sure your points are in the right places: Review your presentation and ensure that points are well placed in an order that makes sense and fits your outline. Great information that is disorganized will not translate into a good presentation.

Create notes using flash cards; these can help you on the day of the presentation: Flash cards are helpful in remembering key points that you will discuss during your presentation. They can also be used to remember quotes and specific facts or statistics. The end result of using flash cards to remember key material is that your audience will realize that you are well prepared and know what you are talking about. This will increase their confidence in the material you are presenting to them. During the presentation you may have the cards handy. In most cases you may not need them; however, it is reassuring to know that should you need to refresh your memory on any points, they are in your hands!

Add appropriate quotes, jokes etc.: In order to spice up your presentation it may be helpful to add quotes or even jokes. This will depend to a great extent on the nature of the presentation and the audience. Be careful not to lose sight of your original objective. Also take note of the audience and be sure to stay clear of comments and jokes that could be deemed offensive.

Choose a template/design to match the topic; be original and inventive: The wonderful part about templates these days is that you will find a vast array from which to make a selection. Be sure to make time to select a template that fits the topic. Your template will be stared at throughout your presentation and it will give an impression to your audience. If you choose the appropriate template, that impression will be a positive one. Experiment with different templates and get opinions from others to ensure that you choose the most appropriate template. For example, if you are presenting on International Business, you could choose a template with a world globe on the top border of each slide. However, you must try out the template to be sure that it is suitable. Some templates may require color adjustments to ensure that your bullet points are actually seen by your audience. Always look at the impact on your presentation when you add all visuals before finally selecting a template. Avoid selecting templates that are commonly used. A thorough search online will reveal a variety of templates that you can choose from. As you become more comfortable with PowerPoint you will even realize that you can design your own templates to match your presentation.

Use visuals/sounds to make your points: The effectiveness of a presentation is positively affected by including the appropriate visuals and sounds. Well selected visuals make it easy to get your audience to understand specific points. They also add to the overall likeability of your presentation. When relevant, you may consider including short video clips or relevant sound bites. For example, in presenting on Dr. Martin Luther King Junior, you may want to include a 60 second sound bite on a speech he made. This may be much more effective than trying to quote the speech yourself. It also alters the presentation for your audience and makes it more interesting.

Use easy to read fonts; Arial/Times New Roman are professional: There are a variety of fonts that can be chosen for your presentation. Be sure to select one that is first and foremost easy to read. At times the most artistic fonts are the most difficult to read and that only hampers your presentation. Your points should be clear to everyone in the audience.

Minimize the number of slides in your presentation; people get bored easily. It is important to stick to your outline and keep the number of slides to the barest minimum. A presentation that is too long will definitely bore your audience and they will lose their focus on the points you are trying to get across. It is helpful to find out in advance the exact amount of time that you will have to present and prepare to utilize that amount of time, and where possible, even less.

Use a good color contrast so that others can read the text in your presentation: You may have prepared the best presentation possible and yet still lose your audience simply because they are unable to read your points due to a bad color contrast. For example, the color of your text should be the opposite in terms of contrast to that of your template background. White text against a dark (or even black) background will allow your points to be easily read.

Write with passion; develop an interesting story: It is better for you to assume that your audience is astute and has some knowledge of the topic. A well prepared presentation shows and your audience will appreciate that. On the other hand, it is not difficult for the audience to identify a presentation that lacked in effort and interest on your part. Develop an interesting presentation based on your interest and research on the topic. It will be appreciated.

A bullet point; that is what it is all about: Presentations in most cases should consist of bullet points. Avoid putting in whole paragraphs or sentences as much as possible. This clutters your presentation while indicating a break from the general rule of presentations: bullet points or power points! The points are there to focus both you and your audience. Your task is to explain those points.

Review, Review, Review!!! Edit your presentation until it feels and looks right: Just like writing, presentations also require editing. As you continue to edit you will identify ways to smoothen the presentation to make it more professional and interesting. The more times you edit your presentation, the better the final product. As you edit you may also experiment with different effects. However, be sure to develop a high level of proficiency in using these special effects in order for them not to adversely impact your presentation. For example, you could include a timer in your presentation. However, this may hamper your ability to slow down and focus on explaining certain points. In such a situation, trying to disable the timer during the presentation may prove difficult. During the presentation, you should be presenting and not tweaking the technology behind the presentation. Such activities should be undertaken well before the presentation.

## 8.3 Preparation for the Actual Presentation

The impression created by those who present very well is that they are presenting effortlessly. Do not be deceived. The best presentations are those that a lot of preparation went into. One of the most interesting presenters in the past was the late Steve Jobs of Apple. His presentation style seemed off the cuff; however, every single point was well rehearsed. Preparing for the presentation is just as important as putting the presentation itself together. It would be a waste to prepare a solid presentation and not present it properly.

Practice the presentation; make sure you go through it several times on your own. As you continue to practice and go through the whole presentation, you will become more comfortable with the material and the timing.

Ask friends to listen to and comment on your presentation: it is helpful to try presenting before friends. This gives you the feel of someone listening to your actual presentation. In addition, you may end up getting useful comments from your friends that could assist you in improving the presentation.

You should also try using a mirror to practice the presentation. Go through the presentation on your own in front of a mirror. This will help you to realize mannerisms that you may need to control as well as portions of your presentation that you may have to improve upon.

Time the whole presentation to ensure that you do not go overboard: A big part of your presentation is the time it will take for you to go through it. By timing an actual dry run you will be able to know well in advance, whether the timing is appropriate. Your aim is to complete the presentation within a specific time frame. Your audience will appreciate it. It is important to stay within the time that you are given to present.

Get familiar with the room; if you are going to present in a venue that you can get access to, make it a point to visit this venue and get a feel for the environment. Check all equipment; Take the time to develop a comfort level with the equipment that you are to use on the presentation day. Many knowledgeable presenters have been made to look rather clumsy and confused because they did not bother to go to the presentation venue early and make sure that they could operate the computer, projector and any other equipment. Remember, every computer is structured in its own unique manner. Make sure that your storage device works with the equipment and that there is internet access if you need it. Be sure to have a backup of your presentation. Where internet access is available you may email the presentation to yourself. If your presentation contains movie clips and sound bites, these may be lost if you email the presentation. You do not need any surprises on the day of the presentation!

Dress well; whether you are asked to or not, make the effort to appear in a business like attire on the day of your presentation. It is a special day so use the opportunity to treat it as such. In addition, people respond to appearances and you will be surprised at the response to a good presentation when you are dressed properly!

Memorize specific quotes etc.; it is important to appear knowledgeable about your subject matter. Quotes that are relevant can assist you to emphasize key points in your presentation. In addition, people respond better to a presentation when they are convinced that the presenter knows the subject matter well.

Get rest the night before; a fresh mind is the best possible ally for a presentation. It will allow you to be comfortable, confident and flexible to adapt to any changes that you may have to make.

## 8.4  Delivering the Presentation

The day has come and you are ready to make your presentation! You want your audience to learn from your presentation and appreciate all the effort that you put into making the presentation. Presenting effectively is like the icing on the cake. The following pointers will assist you in delivering an excellent presentation.

Make a conscience effort to keep your tone and voice upbeat and positive! This has a tremendous impact on how the audience receives your presentation. If you sound bored and disinterested, it will have a negative impact on your audience. You can create enthusiasm for your presentation based on your upbeat and positive tone.

Stick to your outline; do not go off script as you could enter into uncharted territory that could damage the quality of your presentation. Further, deviating from your presentation outline and script could mean taking more time than you were scheduled to use.

Make sure that you start your presentation by introducing yourself and your affiliation. Do not take it for granted that everyone knows exactly who you are. The best presentation should have a sound beginning.

Plan a powerful opener; it is important to catch the crowd's attention as soon as you start your presentation. A simple but appropriate joke may create a relaxed environment amongst your audience and make them more receptive to your presentation.

Be honest and show respect to your audience. This can be seen from how you handle yourself throughout the presentation. The level of preparation that you put into the presentation will also show your audience that you took the presentation seriously. Remember that in all likelihood most of your audience have a decent knowledge of your topic and trying to fake a good presentation may not work.

Be relaxed when presenting, after all the audience consists of people, just like you! You will feel nervous, especially when you start presenting. However, as you continue and follow your script, the preparation will pay off and it will become easier.

If you are too nervous, you can pretend that you are alone or looking at a mirror. In some cases, it may be helpful to focus on the back of the room at a specific point. This gives the impression that you are looking at the audience.

If for any reason you get flustered while presenting; pause and glance down at your flash cards containing your notes. Do not be in a hurry. Remember, you are well prepared and know what you are talking about! The flash cards will help you to stay on point and continue presenting.

If you lose your place during your presentation; move on. By doing so smoothly and without a long delay, no one may even notice!

It is helpful to maintain eye contact with the audience throughout your presentation. Continuously move your eyes around the room and do not focus only on one section. As you continue to present, you will realize that it becomes easier to develop the skill of glancing at your audience. It is an effective way of engaging your audience and letting them know that you are aware of them.

## 8.5  Handling Questions During and After a Presentation

It is important to always have a question and answer period as part of the presentation. Do not shy away from this aspect of the presentation. Given the limited time you had to present, you may not have gone into detail on everything. A question/answer period will allow your audience to obtain further information from you. In addition, there may have been certain aspects of your presentation that require further clarification.

If you are given the option of having a time allotted for questions and comments, please make sure to include this. Questions allow you to shine; they are an opportunity for you to provide additional details that you could not include in your presentation.

There may be some whose questions/comments indicate a different view other than yours on one aspect of the presentation. Do not argue with anyone; be positive and respectful. If there is a difference of opinion, agree to disagree with your reasons for doing so and go on to the next question. Never fall into the trap of arguing about controversial points that can never lead to a peaceful conclusion in that short time. Remember that you have a full audience and the aim is to provide information for all of them and not to solely focus on one person, especially one who disagrees with your views.

Keep your answers to any questions simple and straight to the point. Talking too much can only lead to saying things that can deviate from your key points and at times get you in trouble! Someone in the audience could latch onto a loose statement and this could be embarrassing. In addition, a poorly answered question may cause your audience to doubt the quality and content of your presentation itself. On the other hand, answering questions well shows the audience that you have a good working knowledge of the subject matter. One suggestion is to practice answering questions. You could design questions and ask a friend to deliver them for you to answer. It is not uncommon for some presenters to actually plant people in the audience with specific questions that they have practiced for!

There may be certain questions that you cannot answer. If you do not know the answer to a question, simply say so! No one can terrorize you for saying you do not know a particular point. Lying is not an option. Remember that you need to show respect to your audience at all times. In addition, someone in the audience may realize that you are lying and expose you.

Finally, enjoy the experience of presenting; you are sharing information with others, and it can be fun! You may learn quite a lot from the whole experience and this will help you in future presentations. With time and experience, you will be able to gauge the audience and know when to step on the accelerator or make simple adjustments to ensure that your presentation is well received.

## 8.6 General Do's and Don'ts

The earlier information provided should enable you to prepare a great presentation and present effectively. Following are some general dos and don'ts that you should take note of. Having knowledge of them will increase your chances of making successful presentations.

When it comes to quotes and poetry etc. make sure that they are relevant! Do not include them in your presentation for inclusion sake. Using the right quote can show your command of the subject matter as well as the effort you put into preparing for the presentation.

At all times during your presentation, remember to keep cool, don't lose your head!!! Even if you forget a point, there is always a way to smoothly move on. As you continue to practice and improve your presentation skills, you will find that even your approach to dealing with a mishap will be so smooth that no one even noticed you missed a point!

Make sure that your presentation has a consistent color scheme. At times presenters lose their audience by being too ambitious with colors that just do not work. The most important thing is to be consistent in your color scheme. Also, you want your audience to be able to read what you have put in your slides and the color scheme plays a big role in terms of visibility.

In terms of transitions; remember that less is more. It is important to keep your audience focused on your message. Creating transitions that are too fancy may distract your audience and divert interest from the points that you are trying to make. It is important to use high quality graphics that provide excellent clarity for your presentation. Going through the presentation and trying different effects will give you a chance to choose the most suitable graphics possible.

While it may seem comfortable to do this, please do not read slides word for word; this is boring and everyone can read on their own anyway! You are there to shed light and expand upon the bullet points on your slides.

When presenting it is important to maintain a consistent speed throughout; if you reviewed properly then you will be comfortable knowing that you will be able to finish within the stipulated time. Timing is very important and your preparation in this regard will pay off well.

Make sure that you have reviewed your slides and only depict the final versions! Use slide sorter to review all slides. A common mistake is to lose track of the different versions of your presentation and present using an old version that lacks the clarity and quality work that you have put into your presentation. Double check your files and name them appropriately with dates/ versions etc. to avoid this fatal error. There is no sense in working so hard only to end up presenting an old version of your presentation.

In terms of your physical location, it is important that you position yourself properly. Do no block the presentation at any time. Get out of the way! The audience must be able to see the presentation at all times. That is why you prepared it (the presentation). Do not turn your back to the audience; that is not why they are there, to look at your back! Face them as much as you can.

When possible, prepare handouts for the audience. These should include your PowerPoint slides as well as any other relevant information (especially those that you know would not be covered during your presentation yet are quite relevant). Quality handouts allow your audience to follow your presentation as well as show that you are properly prepared.

Finally, limit punctuation in your presentation and avoid using all capital letters. Review the presentation to ensure that you are consistent in this regard. Remember to use bullet points and not paragraphs or whole sentences.

## 8.7  Getting Rid of the Fear of Presenting

Many people are scared of presenting before a group of people. However, considering the fact that college graduates eventually end up in management roles where leadership skills are required, presenting is a skill that is worthy of excelling in. Each person is different and you may have to try a few techniques before finding the one that works best for you. Remember though that in many cases, the more you present, the more you get comfortable with presenting. It is helpful to seize opportunities to volunteer to present. This means getting your feet wet and becoming more comfortable presenting in front of others. The good old mirror and practice approach are also very helpful. Trying out in front of others is also a very good idea. One can also focus on the back of the room initially. However, with time it is important to periodically change your focus and look at different groups in the crowd.

An important point to note is that you do not need to rid yourself totally of the fear of presenting. The fear is natural and even the most experienced presenters have a fear of presenting. Your task is to minimize the fear so that you do not become paralyzed and unable to present at all. In other words, it is perfectly normal to have anxiety before presenting. The key is to prepare well enough so that the fear is minimized. If you are well prepared you can focus and this will allow you to work through the feeling of fear.

Take all the suggestions in this chapter seriously and you may be on your way to becoming an excellent presenter. You may find the need to modify certain aspects of presenting that work better for you. Feel free to make reasonable adjustments that suit you better. Being nervous means that you will have adrenaline flowing through your system at an increased pace. This energy should be used to ensure that you speak with passion and a vitality that will keep your audience interested in what you are speaking about. In this manner, your nervous energy can then be used to work for you!

Be honest with yourself about your fear, of presenting. It may help if you ask yourself a series of questions. What exactly are you afraid of? Is it the fear of failing? Are there things scarier than the fear of presenting? Definitely! To overcome your fear of presenting it is important to confront your fear and realize that there are many things more frightening than presenting. Further, you can overcome your fear and develop into an excellent presenter. The key is to prepare very well.

There are a few things that you can do to reduce the fear and possible physical manifestations of that fear. You may realize that as time approaches for you to present that your throat may be parched. It is important to drink water to quench your thirst. It is important to use the restroom before the presentation.

The initial fear may also lead to shallow breathing and you can overcome this by making a conscience effort to breath in deeply several times. This will have a calming effect on you as your breathing becomes more normal.

When you are about to start presenting, be sure to make eye contact with different people in the audience. This will calm you and make you realize that you are not alone. Connecting with your audience can have a calming effect on you. Smile a lot and allow the fear to be converted into positive energy. When possible, ask your audience questions. This type of interaction creates a bond between you and the audience. Any positive way that you can connect with your audience will enable you to control your nerves and present to the best of your ability.

Your speaking tone should be positive and upbeat. The audience will feel that energy and that signals to them your desire to connect with them. Be sure to speak in a strong, controlled and slow voice. Your greatest strength as a presenter is to be heard and understood. By speaking slowly and clearly you will avoid rushing and causing your message to be garbled.

For some, presentation fears can be eradicated simply by them pretending that they are speaking only with one person. If this will make you feel more comfortable when presenting, then by all means try it.

Any combination of the above suggestions can assist you to become more comfortable and present effectively. Stick to the basics and do prepare! That will be your ultimate source of confidence, enabling you to present effectively. Most important of all, learn to have fun with presenting. With time and practice you will become an excellent presenter!

"Being ignorant is not so much a shame, as being unwilling to learn." Benjamin Franklin

# 9.0

# Using Technology in the Learning Process

"You learn something every day if you pay attention"
Ray LeBlond

The modern student has access to more technology options than ever. From laptops, notebooks, tablets to smart phones; all these devices create a number of options to enhance the learning process. In earlier sections, some of the uses of technology in the learning process have been suggested.

In this section, technology is looked at with the aim of opening up as many options as possible to students. It may not be exhaustive, but it provides a basis to expand upon. What you should be looking for are the simplest and most effective ways to infuse existing technologies into your learning process.

Available technology today means:

- Faster access to information anywhere and anytime; internet access
- Optional communication tools; emails and twitter, face book etc.
- Social media sites are options for networking with class mates and developing study groups
- Internet access and technology such a Skype mean the ability to set up virtual study groups; groups do not always have to meet physically, which reduces time moving around and cost of transportation
- The ability to take on-line courses

The challenge is to let the technology reflect in your school work in terms of improved quality. Traditionally, a dictionary was always a helpful book to own. These days you can have a dictionary application downloaded and refer to it with ease as a step towards improving your vocabulary. Internet access on various devices means you have loads of information that you can access at your fingertips. In some cases, the issue may be too much information to choose from! If this is ever an issue, remember to focus on the most relevant and self-explanatory materials. You have access to a broad online encyclopedia or library so to speak.

You can access your school library on-line, review e-books and even order certain materials online from your library. Find out the tools and on-line resources that your school provides and determine how you can infuse these into your learning process.

Learning how to use Google effectively is very helpful. Use the key word approach, try different terms, and ask the basic questions such as what, where, how, when and why. If you search in the right manner, you will be able to find just about anything on-line. Remember to note quality on-line resources for future reference by paging them and creating catalogued documents with respective links.

Technology focused strategies that students can use include the following:

- Recording lectures
- Developing flash cards on phones and other devices
- Reviewing flashcards/notes on the phone while on a train or bus to school
- Putting school calendars on phones and other devices
- Getting regular access to news and other periodic information on specific topics

Technology can assist students to organize and modify information. It can make the whole learning process more efficient and interesting. Tools available to students include word processing, database management, design, and graphing software. It is essential to develop a proficiency in using the various tools that are applicable to your courses and future career field. Those who learn how to use the tools effectively seem to fare better academically and spend less time stressing about how to use these technologies. Find out your technology quotient (TQ) and build on your capabilities. It will be a tremendous help not only in school but when you begin working as well. The technology quotient, like an Intelligence Quotient, measures your ability to effectively utilize current software and related applications. You can test your ability to utilize a variety of software by taking an on-line exam. A number of schools also run technology courses that would prepare you before taking any exams.

## 9.1 Core Computer Application Skills for Success:

Microsoft Word; writing reports, assignments and undertaking research; this software improves writing skills with editing features such as spell check etc.

Microsoft Excel; spreadsheets; for computations, basic data, drawing charts, diagrams etc.

PowerPoint; for creating presentations

Database; keeping databases, using them to research and undertake effective analysis.

Windows/other operating systems; knowledge of operating systems enhance your overall computer experience. With time the level of knowledge required in this regard has gone up.

Other areas to cover include creating folders and organizing your materials effectively as well as saving and manipulating files. There are many training programs you can access online to enhance your skills in utilizing spreadsheets, PowerPoint, word processing and other relevant software. A key place to start upgrading your skills in using Word, Excel and PowerPoint amongst others, is the Microsoft Office 365 Training Center.

## 9.2  Emails

Using emails effectively; for example, you can email reports, research and various other documents to yourself and reduce the need to use memory sticks that you could easily lose. You can also use this method as a back-up strategy. In the early days of computers, the golden rule was to back up your work every single day. Many ignore this rule these days and suffer the consequences of wasting time to redo work that they have already completed and subsequently lost. Emails also serve the purpose of enabling prompt communication with others. Check your emails regularly and develop a habit of responding promptly to incoming mails. Remember to note spam and other irrelevant emails so that you do not waste a lot of time cleaning your inbox up in search of serious emails. Most schools provide email accounts for the duration of your course. Be sure to use this account for school purposes mainly. In setting up such accounts avoid using unprofessional names for your email account. This can create the wrong impression about you to others.

## 9.3  Learning Management Systems: Blackboard/Canvas

Blackboard and Canvas are examples of widely used Learning Management Systems (LMS), at the undergraduate and graduate level in many schools. The LMS can be a strong ally in your academic progress if you learn how to use it well. These systems usually give students access to course outlines, PowerPoint presentations for lectures, additional readings for various courses, the school library and e-books, grade center, blogs and other useful tools. Regular access to grade center means that you can have a view of your grades at any point in time. This takes the guessing out of the amount of work you need to do to improve your grades. As most courses indicate the grading system, you can delve deeper and even determine the grades required to obtain an overall A or B+ etc. This should be a strong tool to use in your study planning process. You should be monitoring your performance often. In addition, grade center can assist you to identify any work that you may have missed. This will give you an opportunity to make arrangements to make up such school work and avoid losing precious points. Through monitoring the LMS, you should be able to minimize losing points unnecessarily.

## 9.4 Online Videos

Online videos on many topics exist, find them and view them to buttress your understanding of various topics. For example, if you are studying entrepreneurship, you could check online for video clips of successful entrepreneurs making presentations or being interviewed. Be creative in identifying the manner in which you could use this resource to enhance your learning experience. Such clips and presentations can enhance your learning process and at times are easy to remember if used properly. Make sure that the clips are relevant and that the sources of the clips are reliable. The last thing you want is to utilize unreliable and questionable sources of information. Saving whole clips can take up a lot of space on your computer and you may want to rather list the URL (the address of a website or more specifically the Uniform Resource Locator) in a word document that is appropriately titled. A major location for various instructional videos is YouTube.

## 9.5 Use Technology with Care

Technology can improve efficiency in the learning process. However, it must be used in the proper manner to gain positive results. For example, in India, it is common for grade schools and high schools to ban the use of calculators by students. This policy has some impact on the performance of students. The aim of the policy is to enhance the mental capabilities of students to process math and other related materials. The result is what we are all witness to; an Indian labor force that is very competent in the technology field worldwide. These kinds of strategies may seem insignificant to some, however the results can be tremendous! If you can improve certain memory skills such as the ability to undertake mental calculations by minimizing the use of calculators, then by all means do so. Do not allow technologies to reduce your mental capabilities.

## 9.6 Smartphone Applications

There are many educational applications that have been designed and created for Smart phones. These can be of great assistance to students and when possible should be utilized to maximize overall academic performance. One of these is iStudiez Pro. This educational app allows a student to better control their schedule. Tasks that can be undertaken with the app include tracking assignments, posting deadlines for various academic activities and getting assignment deadline alerts. The app is available for $2.99.

The following are various apps that can assist in the learning process.

### BenchPrep Companion

This app assists students in preparing for major exams such as GMAT (Graduate Management Admission Test), GRE General Test, and LSAT (Law School Admission Test). Features in the app include study plans, practice questions and flashcards.

The app is available in ITunes or directly from the publishers' website. There is a subscription fee charged for use of the app.

### Brainscape

This app utilizes modern flash card technology to assists students in creating their own flash cards or utilizing existing ones for various courses. The app focuses on scientific methods to create learning tools that enhance studying.

The app is available either for a monthly subscription or a onetime fee.

### Chegg

This app allows students to rent or buy textbooks. It also provides assistance with homework as well as access to tutors. The app also has a feature to assist students with Math by providing step by step solutions. There are various charges and they depend on the services one chooses to use.

### CliffsNotes Study Guides

This app provides a study guide for an array of courses including literature, accounting algebra, and math. The app also includes Test Preparation materials for GRE, GMAT and PRAXIS.

The app comes with a fee dependent on the selection of materials chosen.

### Dictionary.com, Merriam-Webster, or Oxford Dictionary

There are various dictionary apps available for download. It may be worth comparing them and determine the one that best suits your needs. Most of these apps are free to download and use.

### Duolingo

This app assists students to learn how to speak, read and write other languages. The approach utilized is through the creation of fun systems that make learning languages as easy as a game experience. The app is free to use.

### EasyBib

This app assists in citing research references and includes a number of citation styles such as APA, Chicago and MLA.

### Evernote

This app is a note taking one that allows one to capture ideas, notes and lists. It also allows for an interphase with ones' computer and other technology devices. The app is free to use.

### iTunes U

ITunes U has a wide array of audio and video files of free lectures, books and other learning materials from universities and public organizations worldwide. The app is free.

### LitCharts

This app helps students to understand literature. There are reviews, summaries and quotes for a large number of titles. The app is free.

### Microsoft Office Mobile

This app allows one to have access to well used programs such as Word, Excel and PowerPoint as well as other Microsoft Office products. The app requires a subscription. One can use the app to store documents in the cloud and have access to them from various devices.

### RealCalc Scientific Calculator

This is a downloadable scientific calculator with all the functions of an orthodox calculator. The app is free.

### Left to Spend

This app is a basic one for budgeting. It allows one to input all expenses and provides information on how much one has to spend. The app also allows for the creation of charts to determine where your money is going. The app basically allows for a simple overview of ones' finances.

### Scholly

Scholly allows one to find scholarships for college and graduate schools as well as track scholarship applications. It also allows one to proofread and enhance scholarship essays. The app is $2.99 per month.

### Venmo

This app allows one to split bills and transfer/receive money easily to/from others as well as to make purchases. It is a digital wallet.

### MyFitness Pal

This app allows one to record all food intake as well as exercise regimes. The app is free.

### Wholesome

This app allows one to find simple food recipes. It is also a vitamin and micronutrient tracker. Health scores are provided for the recipes. The app is free.

### Dashlane

This app allows one to safely store all passwords and personal information. Given the wide array of passwords that one has to track and remember, this is a very useful app that can make life that much easier for a student. The app is free, though there are premium editions that come at a monthly subscription.

There are many more apps that can assist in making life more organized while one is in school. It is very much worth it to explore and identify those that can be of assistance in your academic journey. One can speak with classmates to find out about other apps that they use to assist them in school and compare which ones are most helpful. Be adventurous in your search. Apps can be found for free/cheap entertainment, shopping, transportation, accommodation and a variety of other activities.

"I don't think much of a man who is not wiser today than he was yesterday" Abraham Lincoln

# 10.0

# Exam Room Strategies

"Experience is a dear teacher, but fools will learn at no other."
Benjamin Franklin

The exam room is the battleground and you are the superhero! You have to have a plan for the battle before you enter the exam room. The exam time is limited and must be utilized wisely. It would be a shame to study hard only to go into the exam room and have a myriad of problems beset you that lead to a low grade. With a well laid out plan prior to the exam, you will minimize the chance of this happening, if not eliminate it totally. Do not take it for granted that studying alone will bring you the desired results. Be well prepared on all fronts.

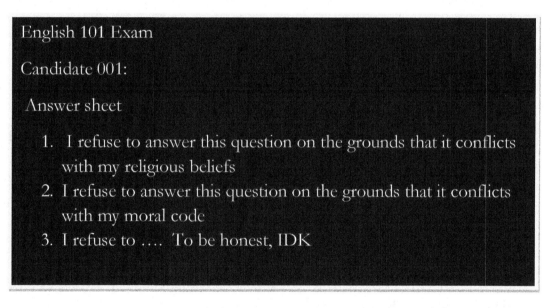

English 101 Exam

Candidate 001:

Answer sheet

1. I refuse to answer this question on the grounds that it conflicts with my religious beliefs
2. I refuse to answer this question on the grounds that it conflicts with my moral code
3. I refuse to …. To be honest, IDK

**English 101 Exam responses**

## 10.1 Before the Exam

Before every exam there are a series of steps you can utilize to develop an effective exam plan. It is normal in many cases to be told details about the pending exam. You should seek out and note all the information given. This is what you will use to plan your exam strategy.

Typical information about the exam could include:

- The date of the exam and the time the exam will start
- The length of the exam is usually given (for example 2 hours or three hours etc.)
- The exam method, be it multiple choice or essays or fill-ins is also normally given
- The number of questions in the exam
- The maximum number of points for each question

For illustration purposes, let us take the following scenario for an exam that you are to take in the near future:

Sample Examination Information:

The date is March 1st and time is 9am – 12 noon and the exam method is essay questions.

The number of questions to be answered in all will be five (5) and each question is worth 20 points.

A well prepared time management plan will ensure the following:

- That you will be confident as you follow the plan
- That you will be organized
- That points will not be forgotten
- That the plan will allow for a review time to edit your responses as well as make sure that you actually answered the questions.
- That you will be able to apportion a reasonable amount of time to each question.
- That you will not go overboard on one question and risk not completing the exam
- You will be able to answer the number of questions the exam requires. You then have a chance to obtain as high a grade as possible. Remember, if one has to answer 5 questions, worth twenty points each, answering only 3 questions for example will give a maximum grade of about 60%, which in most schools is an F!

## 10.2  Typical Exam Room Plan:

a. Question review – first 5 - 10 minutes

The first thing you need to do is to read any instructions that are given. After this, you should then read the questions. During the first 5 minutes of the exam, your plan is to review all the instructions as well as the questions. After you have understood the instructions, go on to read the questions. Familiarize yourself with the questions and get a feel for what is required. You can read through the questions quickly first, then much slower the second time. This ensures that you do not overlook parts of questions.

The question review period should be used for question selection as well if you are for example given 10 questions and have to answer only 5 of them. How do you choose the right questions? Your job is to select the questions that you are best prepared for. You can test this by preparing a marking scheme or your selected questions. This scheme is basically a summary of all the key points that should be included in your answer. A review of your marking scheme will enable you to identify the questions you are most equipped to answer.

If you are allowed to answer the questions in any order, it is important to answer the questions you know best first. Find out, before the exam if possible whether you will be allowed to do this. Once the questions have been selected, it may be helpful to underline and note key instructions and points required for each question. This enables a thorough assessment and identification of the exact answers required for each question. It will assist in ensuring that your focus is on the actual points required to answer the questions.

By answering the questions that you are best prepared for first, you give a good impression of yourself to the examiner. In addition, some may only read the first questions into detail and if you answered the first ones well, they tend to give you a benefit of the doubt and scan the last questions looking for key points. Starting with your worst answers will do the opposite!

b. Developing structure of the answer for each question – Marking Scheme 5 -10 minutes

In other words, prepare a bullet pointed scheme (I call this a marking scheme) including all the key points that you would have to discuss for each question. Ask yourself, what does the Professor want in terms of information for each question? The following is a marking scheme for a sample question:

## 10.3 Sample Question and Corresponding Marking Scheme:

Following is a sample exam question along with the proposed answer or marking scheme. This is the ultimate outline that can ensure a focused and well organized answer to an exam question.

**Identify and discuss issues that make managing a business today more challenging than yesterday:**

Sample Marking Scheme

Proposed Answer:

    a. Introduction; In the past the environment was not as complicated, easier to maneuver than now

    b. Key Points:

    a. Technology, the internet and computer hardware and software

    b. Globalization and diversity

    c. Bigger and more complex organizational structures

    d. Diversity of job functions to monitor

    e. Diagrams/charts

    f. Equations

    g. Main quotes/ key phrases etc.

    c. Conclusion; A summary of your key points with your opinions, if relevant

Prepare the above type of marking scheme for every single question that you have to answer. The biggest advantage of this marking scheme is that once you put down the key points for each question, you will not forget them! All you will be doing for the rest of the exam is expanding on the written down points in your marking scheme.

    c. Time for answering the five questions – 30 minutes each

Follow your marking scheme and carefully explain each point to the best of your ability. In an essay exam, using bullet points is not recommended. The essay questions seek to ascertain your level of knowledge of the subject matter amongst other things. By carefully constructing paragraphs based on your key points (within your marking scheme), you stand a better chance of addressing all the important points and getting a higher grade.

You are also being graded indirectly on your ability to follow instructions. Monitor the time as you go along. Some students acquire a clock just for exams and it makes it easy for them to glance at it and monitor the time they spend with each question. This allows you to ensure that you stay within the time frame for each question. Do not spend more than the planned time on any one question. Your objective should be to answer every single question to ensure you get a chance to get the highest grade possible.

    d. Time for review of all answers – 10 minutes

Use this time to read through your answers. You will be surprised at the amount of improvements via editing that you will be able to make. In some cases, you will even realize the need to squeeze in forgotten points! Do not leave the exam room early, use the allotted time fully to your advantage. A good review of your answers can make the difference between an A and a B+!

Edit your answers as neatly as possible. Remember that someone has to read your answers to award you marks! While the review exercise may seem boring, it is advisable to do it and ensure that you have provided complete responses for a maximum grade. Your biggest motivating factor should be the possibility of an excellent grade!

When editing your answers, look out for the following in particular:

- Check that you have put your name and all other required information on the exam paper/booklet
- All questions were answered
- All pages were numbered properly
- All diagrams and formulae were put in the essays at the right places
- All diagrams and formulae are properly labeled
- If you use diagrams or formulae, make sure that you refer to them; there must be a reason for using them and it is up to you to indicate exactly why or clearly explain the point you are trying to make with them. You can and should practice the above.

## 10.4 Anticipating and Preparing for Specific Questions

Before the exam, take a look at each chapter that you have covered. What were the most critical points that you learnt? What questions have appeared in previous exams/ assignments? Use all of this information to design your own exam paper. Then set up the exam time management scheme and allot time for answering the questions under exam like conditions. Go ahead and write the simulated exam. After, review your answers using your textbook and notes. Assess how well you did. You can try changing the questions and going through this exercise several times. The more times you do this, the more you will be prepared for the final exam. By varying the questions, you limit the chances of seeing a question that you are not prepared for!

The sample exam material I have provided is for an essay examination. However, each professor can and will decide on what exam method they choose to use. Regardless of the method, your job is to modify the exam time management method described and have a plan for what you will be doing during every minute of the exam. You can adjust the time management strategy to any type of exam method.

One of the mental blocks for many students is the issue of varying exam methods. Some students claim that they do better in multiple choice exams for a number of reasons. I have tested this during my teaching years and found this to be false. In fact, students did worse with multiple choice exams than with essays. This result was interesting so I decided to investigate further why many students prefer multiple choice exams, yet fared poorly in them. My enquiries revealed that the reason students liked multiple choice was the fact that at least they knew that somewhere amongst the answers provided, one of them was correct. In addition, some students were honest to admit that they felt a sense of accomplishment with multiple choice exams; even if they had not studied they were able to shade some answers! In the first place, the fact that the answer is amongst the five does not ensure that you will get it right. Only one thing will do that, and that is solid preparation. Further, the satisfaction of shading all of the questions is not your ultimate objective. You want to get a good grade. Feeling good about shading is not necessarily the same thing. You can, of course, do well in a multiple choice just like any other exam. Simply prepare well and you would be more confident instead of guessing. Exams are not meant for guessing, but for showing what you have prepared for and actually know!

With multiple choice examinations some strategies in the exam room can assist in ensuring success:

- You can look for multiple choice exams on your course and use them to practice under exam like conditions. This will condition your mind for the real deal
- You can eliminate the most outrageous answers and eventually have only perhaps 2 answers to choose from
- At times information provided in previous questions actually tip off the answer to following questions
- Grammar is a key step in tricking students in multiple choice questions. Careful reading to note grammar and other oddities can go a long way in ensuring that you are able to identify the correct answers

Ultimately, quality preparation gives you the state of mind that regardless of the method of examination or the questions asked, you will do well because you are prepared! This is what you should be aiming for. With this attitude, regardless of the exam method, you will be calm and focused to do well! Remember, it is ok to pause and gather yourself during an exam as many times as you need to, however, monitor the time as you go along and follow your time management plan.

## 10.5 After the Exam

The period immediately following an exam is a different experience for each person. However, once you are finished, you basically have to let it go and think of other things, perhaps the next exam. One major cause of confusion for many students is the post exam discussions. These discussions at times allow you to listen to the views of others on what the various questions required. If you listen in to such discussions and hear a point or two that you did not mention, or an answer that is different from yours, it could send you into panic mode. Once the exam is over there is nothing more you can do. Discussing and worrying over the exam is an exercise in futility. The exam grades will come out soon enough. As mentioned earlier, you could rather focus on other pending exams. In avoiding post exam discussions, you give yourself an opportunity to have a free mind to prepare for your other exams.

The steps outlined for developing your exam plan are all time related. The calculations get simpler as you practice, especially if the questions are not many.

The following is the summary of a Time Management Plan for a three-hour essay exam that requires you to answer five questions in all:

**Total Minutes for exam: 3hours * 60 minutes = 180 minutes**

| | | |
|---|---|---|
| a. | Reading Instructions and Questions: | 10 minutes |
| b. | Preparing Marking scheme for each question: | 10 minutes |
| c. | Answering each question   @ 5 | 30 minutes |
| d. | Reviewing and editing all answers | 10 minutes |
| **Total time utilized** | | **180 minutes** |

While you should modify your time to suit yourself, make sure that you give adequate time for each phase of the exam to ensure a consistent and solid performance.

"Those that won't be counseled can't be helped." Benjamin Franklin

# 11.0

# Handling Academic Stress: Balancing your Lifestyle with your Course

"If you know how to spend less than you get, you have the philosopher's stone."
Benjamin Franklin

Stress is an unfortunate part of life. When handled well its negative impact can be minimized, if not, negated. Ignoring stress or choosing not to deal with it will not make it go away. Take control of the situation and you will be much better off. One of the chief causes of academic stress is a feeling of being overwhelmed by the amount of work that one has to accomplish. The key point here is that with good planning, this type of stress is seriously minimized as you recognize that you are consistently taking steps to achieve your overall academic goals. When things look clearly workable, you feel more confident and less stressed.

Academic stress may exist even if you manage your time well and study consistently. However, I have learnt that depending on the level of preparation, each person's level of stress is different. For example, I recall going towards an exam room to write an exam and being stressed out. It was the kind of nervous stress that is very normal and comes with simply knowing that you have to write an exam. This type of stress, if managed well is actually good for you! At the same time, you may notice someone looking very nervous prior to an exam. Do not be surprised to find out that that person had missed most of the lectures during the semester and was ill prepared to say the least! That kind of stress is not good and is definitely avoidable!

In many courses, one will realize that the nature of your course comes with its own unique stress. For example, medical students have a grueling schedule that at times dictates that they write exams every single week. Law students may have fewer exams but a lot of cases and materials that must be read within limited time periods. That does not mean that some courses are easy because they do not write an exam every week. It is not fruitful to compare courses in this manner. It is more important to recognize the stress points for your particular courses. Then you can make the necessary adjustments to take account of each course and its requirements.

One key approach that brings down stress especially the day of the actual exam, is to decide on a period before the exam when you simply put all the books and materials away and relax yourself. The relaxation method depends on you; it could be a time to do some exercise, listen to music or simply relax in bed and allow your mind to wander on anything but the exam. Doing this for even 10 minutes can seriously lower your stress level. The rationale behind using such a strategy the day of the exam, is because it is on this day that you have to perform and you want to give your mind the best chance to succeed. Bringing stress down before an exam could be the tonic you need to do your best.

## 11.1  Good Stress?

I mentioned that stress can be good. Being stressed weeks before an exam can motivate you to spend more time reading. That is always good. In addition, many people confess that when they are stressed, especially days or weeks before an exam, it seems to enhance their level of absorption and comprehension. That is the kind of stuff that you should look for. You can actually utilize your stress weeks and days before the exam to motivate you to read consistently and assimilate as much as you can. Ultimately, all the reading and preparation will give you confidence and actually equip you to do well in your exams. As you continue to prepare, your stress level will fall.

Occasionally, I provide my students with questionnaires to find out the key issues that they are concerned about during the course of the academic year. According to the results of these surveys, the following are some of the key issues that bother most students in order of importance:

- Financial commitments
- Work commitments
- Family commitments
- Course commitments

**Library**

During the academic year, it is clear that your school work will bring stress of its own. Your key objective should be to do well in school. As a result, it is imperative that you block out as much as possible any other sources of stress. In a way, the time that you spend in school is similar to having a girlfriend that requires a lot of your time. Having other stresses is like having multiple girlfriends; either you will be caught or the time you spend stressing on the other issues will affect your academic performance adversely. It takes discipline, focus and sacrifice to do well in your various courses. Be prepared to deny yourself of some things to get the academic results you want. In making sacrifices, remember that it is a means to an end. Doing well in your academics will assist you in your professional endeavors. Further, this means not having to flunk out of courses and spend more time and money doing them again. Finally, students who do well in their courses have very low academic stress! This is because doing well in school gives such students a positive boost to their overall confidence and this often can overflow to other aspects of their lives.

## 11.2  Financial Commitments and Money Management

Most students have to face the issue of financial stress. Financial commitments are a source of worry at a time when most students have limited time, if any to work. Bills may abound but the means are in most cases quite limited. It takes a concerted effort for a student to manage their finances well in school.

Perhaps being broke during your school days can be made into a positive situation. Consider the fact that there are basic principles that have to be followed for financial success. The earlier that you learn these principles the more successful you will be in minimizing financial stress. Your student days may be the best time to learn some basic financial principles. The first of these is the concept of budgeting. One must learn how to budget and live within your means. Planning how you will spend your stipend, income or allowance is an important lesson that will last a lifetime. If you are unaware of how to go about developing a budget and following it, go online and Google the topic. There are many sources of free information on budgeting. In addition, the books on the topic are numerous. The concept of budgeting and good money management is considered to be so important that some schools even have non-credit courses to educate students about these matters. Popular topics that you may consider learning about, apart from budgeting include credit management, saving and investments.

As part of your budgeting process, you may want to list down all the items that you spend your money on during a semester. For example, you will have to buy books, school supplies, clothing, toiletries and food. Estimate how much you spend on each item on a monthly basis. Total the amount and compare this to your expected inflows. If your expenditure is less than your income, then you are in good business and headed towards a budget surplus. This means you will have money left over each month after making all required expenditures. If, on the other hand your expenditure exceeds your expected income then you are headed towards a budget deficit and this will definitely bring an enormous amount of stress. You will end up spending quite a bit of time worrying and trying to figure out how you will deal with the situation.

It may be helpful to set up a spreadsheet that you can use regularly to maintain a record of your income and expenditures. The advantage of using a spreadsheet is the fact that you can put in the spreadsheet basic formulae that will automatically add up your figures and let you know your situation at any point in time. Further, by maintaining accurate records you will be able to recognize trends that can assist you in making adjustments to your budget that can help you save more and/or spend less. Appendix 3 provides a basic budget format that you may consider utilizing to maintain your budget records. Make it a point to update this budget as often as necessary.

To deal with a budget surplus, you will have to implement a major financial principle for success, saving! Your wisest option would be to put aside the surplus money into a saving account and keep adding to this account over time. The amount saved can act as a contingency fund that can be used to take care of unplanned expenditures and emergencies. In addition, if you do not have any emergencies, this fund can serve you well in the future when planning expenditures.

Dealing with a budget deficit requires a totally different approach. You will need to review your planned expenditures and rate them in order of importance. List the most important items first. At the top of your expenditure list should be items such as food, books, rent etc. The next step is to cut out items on the bottom of your list that are not of importance. After doing this, recalculate your expenditure and note whether you still have a budget deficit or not. If you still have a budget deficit, then it is important to revisit the items on your list and ask yourself whether all of them are absolutely necessary. Identify further items that you can cut away from your budget. I would recommend that you then look critically at the amounts you estimated for the essential items on your list. It is time to look at cost saving strategies to minimize your expenditure on the essential items. For example, if your rent is too high, you may want to investigate cheaper housing options. Look at your food budget and critically assess the possibility of reducing your expenditure by buying simple, easy to prepare food items as opposed to eating out a lot. You may want to eat simple, healthy and basic meals while in school. Food and rent could comprise a big percentage of your overall budget while in school. Eating takeout meals should definitely be an occasional activity and not a regular one. A high expenditure on food can add up and is a major reason why many students are not able to balance their budgets. Look for good value purchases when you go out food shopping and make it a point to shop regularly for food. After all you will have to eat regularly to survive! Learning how to cook basic dishes may be a good idea to assist you in minimizing your food bill.

Books are another major expenditure. Check all your options for acquiring your school textbooks. Find out whether you can rent books. This is a new and sure method of reducing your textbook bill. Also investigate the possibility of utilizing international textbook editions of the required text for different courses. Before doing this, you may want to speak with you professors and determine the extent to which you will be able to undertake the course without buying the key textbook. Some international editions are simplified and may not have all the details that exist in the main text. Another option is to buy older editions of the textbook. However, here again you have to be careful. While you may save a lot of money, you may have a challenge keeping up with the class because you are continuously checking to see whether your edition has the required material. In this era of tablets, notebooks and powerful cell phones, you may want to explore the idea of buying e-books as opposed to hard copies. They tend to be relatively cheaper than the physical books. Find out from your classmates the options for acquiring the books at cheaper prices. By sharing information, you may find different ways to cut your textbook bill by a significant percentage. Please be careful not to compromise on quality of materials that could adversely impact your academic success.

In making a budget you will have to plan for entertainment even if the amount is small. The biggest task you will have while in school is to identify cheap and at times free sources of entertainment. Surprisingly, if you are prepared to try different activities you will find an amazing amount of things to do that are either free or cost very little. An excessive level of expenditure on entertainment is also a major reason why some students are not able to live within their means.

One of the interesting aspects of college/university life is the easy access to credit cards. It is important from an early stage to understand credit fully before you start using cards. Not having a credit card at all has its disadvantages. Getting one puts you at risk of mismanaging it. Simply put you should understand that using a credit card is tantamount to obtaining a short-term loan. While you may use the credit card to pay for certain items like books or food, the major principle you should follow is to pay off the full amount by the end of the month. If you follow this principle, then you will be on your way to managing credit effectively. In addition, your credit rating will continue to be positive. These days it is common to see ads on TV about a young person who is finding it difficult to acquire a mortgage or a car loan because of bad credit. While the ads may look funny, I can assure you that the problems created by mismanaging credit as a student are very real and serious.

Consider the fact that many companies will rush to your campus and set up tables to offer credit cards. At the same time, these companies will offer free gifts in exchange for your credit card application. A major issue you should note here is that you basically do not need more than one credit card. Having one credit card will make it easier for you to manage your credit as well as minimize the chances of misuse. The fact that many students default on their credit cards should make one ask, why then do companies continue to offer credit cards to students who will default? The reason is simple. By virtue of the high interest rates for defaulting, many companies actually make more money from cards that are defaulted on. Further, these companies also know that eventually a student who has defaulted will realize that without cleaning up their credit and paying past bills, they will not be able to buy a car, a home or at times even pass a credit check for a job! Once you are within the country and planning to live and work in the U.S. then know that all your credit information will be stored and can be used against you. Consider also the fact that while it may take weeks to spoil your credit, it can take years of sacrifice to clean it up. There is no quick fix for repairing credit and it still comes back to paying up. Manage your credit well and avoid all the above messy situations. Keep track of all expenditures that you use your credit card for and make sure to pay off these amounts within a 2-4-week period to avoid late fees.

If you ask yourself some serious questions, it will enable you to refocus yourself and minimize the stress from non-academic factors. Financial commitments are a common stress factor for many people, not just students. In talking with different people I have come to find out that the general thinking is that when you are in school, especially as a full time student, one should expect to live frugally. In doing so you recognize that you can't make much money, if any at all, because of school commitments. As a result, financial stress can be minimized by living within your means and denying yourself. By doing so there is not much stress that finances can bring you. Many students work extra hours before becoming full time students. This is to save as much money as possible, knowing the sacrifice that they have ahead. This is the way to go. I have often heard some students complain that the requirements of school mean they cannot have a life. Well, the reality is that the process of getting higher education involves sacrifice and few, if any, are able to live exciting carefree lives during that period. I always remind students that the school period is not forever. In addition, when one successfully completes their course and gets a job, their lifestyle can then be structured to include all they missed and more!

## 11.3  Work and School

Work commitments should be minimized as much as possible during the academic year. Some employers give special leave to allow students to study for finals. It does not pay to work extra hours and make more money only to fail your courses. I often tell my students that not doing well in school is like standing outside in the snow and throwing your money in the air for anyone to collect! Once you have paid to be in school, do everything possible to get the most out of it, especially completing your course and graduating! If you must work, look for possible techniques to make up the work you have to complete for school. I recall periods when I had to work and also had school assignments to complete or studying to do. One sacrifice I made was to study during lunch breaks. I would have short lunches at my desk and use the rest of the lunch break to study. I also found out that reading flash cards on the train ride was very effective! Sometimes I tried using recorded notes to revise as well. Choose any method that suits you, but be prepared to go the extra mile to overcome the deficit in your time created by working. If you must work and study it means you must be more disciplined and much more time oriented. This is not impossible to do. Always remember your ultimate objective and use this as motivation.

## 11.4 Family and School

Family commitments can be complicated. The situation will vary from person to person. For many, support of the family is just what they need to perform well in school. It is worth letting family members know that you are focused on school during the semester and may not be available for the usual family engagements in all instances. With a good study plan there should be a way to include a few family commitments without harming your overall efforts to do well in school. It is advisable to make your family aware of your focus on school; they can give you support and encouragement!

## 11.5 Friends and School

Friends may also want a piece of your time. If they are not in school like you, then you will have to draw the line and let them know of your objective. I have met some students who told me that they had to drop some friends because the friends were actually hostile towards their academic goals and seemed to do as much as they could to distract them. This is an unfortunate but all too common reaction. The friends are scared of losing you! In some cases, friends may be intimidated by the effort you are making to improve your life. If you want to accomplish things for yourself then you may have to minimize interaction with those who seek to thwart your progress. In fact, you may be better off surrounding yourself with people with similar objectives who would positively motivate you.

## 11.6 Stay Healthy!

There is a lot to be said for a steady exercise regime. Physical health is one key way to support your academic efforts. People who eat and sleep well are less likely to fall ill.

In addition, students who maintain steady exercise regimes indicate that they felt more alive and were able to work more and sleep less as a result of the exercise regime that they followed. Remember that by staying healthy you minimize the chances of missing classes due to illness. Any time that you miss from class can never be recovered. A healthy eating habit will keep you in school and provide you with the strength to take care of your course commitments. In addition, by learning at an early stage how and what to eat to maintain good health, you can avoid the situation of gaining significant weight and then spending years trying to get rid of it. This seems to be a trend in recent times as judged by shows such as the Biggest Loser and commercials showing popular celebrities who joined one diet plan or another and lost a significant amount of weight. Getting a degree is an investment that requires years of your life. You might as well be in a position to enjoy the fruits of your labor long after sacrificing to get your degree(s).

## 11.7  Socialization in School

Social interaction during the academic year with classmates and friends can be healthy if controlled and regulated. There are many positives to being able to unwind for brief periods before or after hitting the books. It is important to have your own ways of relaxing and having fun in school. Whether it is playing computer games or joining the school basketball team, activities such as these keep you balanced. When you need to relax and socialize, feel free to do so. Just make sure you don't binge on it! In addition, do not impugn on other people's time when they are studying. If you respect other peoples time, they will respect yours as well.

In a nutshell when you are in school, minimize outside involvement and focus on your course. By preparing and following your study plan, you can include time for relaxing that will refresh you and ensure a nice balance. That is exactly what you need. You can have fun, just be disciplined about it.

"He that waits upon fortune is never sure of a dinner." Benjamin Franklin

# 12.0

# Conclusion

"We are all born ignorant, but one must work hard to remain stupid."
Benjamin Franklin

Today, many workers are returning to the classroom. How many of these students are doing well? By all indications, not enough of them are excelling in school. Some are not doing so well because they have not been in school for a while and are rusty. In addition, when they were in school such students failed to develop good plans and strategies. As a result, these students lack a positive track record to go back to. Others are not sure how to develop effective study strategies. Unfortunately, a number of those not doing well, keep it a secret and do not let the right people who can advise them know about it. Considering the cost and time required to complete a degree/diploma program it is important to get the most out of the experience.

## 12.1 Golden Rules for Academic Success

Academic success is a worthy goal and you can achieve it! Your success in school may have many positive ramifications for your professional life. Throughout this text, a number of important aspects of the academic process have been discussed and many suggestions have been provided. Below are a number of golden rules that may assist you to achieve your academic objectives:

- Start from the first day of school and make sure you stay focused: Every single day that you delay in getting organized expands the possibility of not meeting your academic targets.
- Prepare a study plan as soon as possible and do all you can to follow it! Plan properly how you will use your time and allow for all aspects of your life to be included such as a time to watch a movie or undertake any other activity of leisure. Once your study plan is well balanced you will be surprised how well you can undertake school work and still have time for other nonacademic activities.
- Study in peaceful environments; your efficiency will increase: For most people a peaceful environment would be a quiet place without much, if any disturbance. Such environments allow for increased concentration. Determine the ideal places

for studying and make sure to use them. If the library is your ideal environment, then use it as your study base. Others are able to study effectively in their dorm room. Whatever your choice is, let it be just that; your choice of an optimal learning environment.

- Maintain good relationships with your faculty and classmates. You will be interlinked with both groups for a while and the earlier you get to know them the better. Form study groups that actually work!

- Spend quality time on assignments; it will build up your knowledge: The typical student either starts working on assignments late or does not spend quality time working on assignments. In most cases, lazy work will attract lazy grades.

- Socialize and take reasonable breaks when you need to; diminishing returns is real. A well balanced study plan should include not only academic commitments but social ones as well. Moderation is the key. It is not uncommon to hear of students who emphasized too much on their social lives only to flunk out of their course.

- Speak up in class and ask questions: You paid a lot of money to be in the class and when you do not understand one thing or another, let your Instructor know. It would be amazing that you would have no questions at all during a lecture/class.

- If you go off your study plan, get up, brush yourself off and regroup. The study plan is a guide for you to follow. At times you may realize that for a day or two you have not followed the study plan. As disturbed as you may feel, the best thing to do is to revert back to the plan. It is important however to minimize the instances when this happens. The closer you stick to the plan the better off you will be.

- If you need help such as tutoring, go out and get it: Let your desire for success include the reality that you may need help at times. If you do, reach out for it! Most academic programs have tutoring components and you are paying for it one way or another, whether you utilize the services or not.

- Read, read, and read! There is no substitute for reading. The more time you spend reading relevant materials, the more you learn.

- Avoid excuses and determine reasons for not doing well so you can address them. Be honest with yourself and take corrective action when necessary to ensure that you continuously improve your performance.

- Monitor your academic progress with a view to improving it consistently. Put in place a monitoring system to ensure that you always know how well you are doing. This will be the best way to practically gauge the changes or extra effort you need to put in place to improve your academic performance.

- Make use of all relevant course materials that you are provided with: Booklists, course outlines, PowerPoint's and other course materials are not given out for the sake of it. Make sure to utilize all the given materials to support your learning process.

- Attend classes enough to get an attendance award! If possible, make it a point not to miss a single class. By attending regularly, you will not have the need to consult others about material you missed. It is also a key step towards staying on track for good grades. Remember to stay focused not only by going to class but also by actually listening well and learning in class as well.

- Develop a good sleeping pattern; your brain works best with regular rest. Sleep is so important for your academic work and getting enough of it can make a huge difference in your academic life.

- Work consistently to avoid not sleeping for days before an exam: Life can be much easier if you prepare on a regular basis as opposed to lazing about for most of the semester and trying to cram loads of material into a short period of time such as a week before finals. Cramming produces stress that could hinder your efforts at effectively absorbing material.

- Eat healthy and exercise. With good health you will have the energy to study and undertake other activities. By taking care of yourself and staying healthy you avoid losing days/weeks due to illness.

## 12.2 Monitoring and Improving your Performance

As soon as you start your courses, set up a spreadsheet that you can use to input and monitor all exam, project and assignment results. From semester to semester you can then view individual results for each course as well as your overall GPA (Grade Point Average). Any declines that you identify in your grades should act as signals for you to determine the need to make prompt changes in your study plan for better results.

Pinpoint the factors that led to a poor academic performance in any course. Be ready to be critical of your efforts in a bid to identify the key factors. The reasons for your poor performance can then credibly form the basis for any changes or adjustments that you would like to make.

Remember that improving or maintaining a strong GPA could have positive financial implications. Some schools provide scholarships for students with exceptional grades. In addition, many employers utilize GPA levels of potential employees to identify the best of the best.

Does music have a neutral or positive impact on your reading and study skills? The answer is no. The impact of music is negative! Studies of the brain show that those who read with music are actually giving the brain more work to do and in effect reducing their overall comprehension capability. The brain works on moving the music to the background while also trying to comprehend what you are reading. Almost like a computer, you are unnecessarily overloading the brain, so expect less comprehension. If you want the maximum level of concentration, simply put the music off while you are trying to study!

If necessary, one may decide to seek outside counsel on how to deal with improving one's performance. Faculty, learning centers and seniors can all provide inputs on how to tackle pesky courses. Faculty members have dealt with many students and have knowledge that is waiting to be tapped. When you recognize the need for outside assistance do not leave any stone unturned to get such help. Your classmates should be an excellent starting point for you. The earlier you start networking and socializing with your classmates the better for you. However, make sure that you are prepared to assist others as well. The academic process is not a one-way street. Developing a positive reputation for assisting others can lead to others being prepared to assist you. Just make sure you do not slip from your plans as a result of assisting others. Ironically, assisting others with their academic work can positively reinforce materials that you have covered.

The learning process and strategies to attain academic success are many and varied. In my opinion each student should find out what is out there in terms of options and select those strategies that work best for them.

The key to academic success is reading, and a whole lot of it! This can't be avoided. The earlier you start inculcating that habit, the better off you will be. Yes, sacrifices need to be made and discipline must be instituted to ensure that you develop your plan and stick to it.

There will be times when you will go off the plan. Do not let these times drag on or else they could spell your doom. Revise your schedule and plans to take account of times when you do go off your plan. It is not a crime to go off your schedule, but it could be disastrous not to minimize such times and change your game plan accordingly.

Set goals to accomplish each semester. One may ask; how high should I aim? My suggestion is that you should aim as high as possible! By doing so, if you miss your initial target grade at least you may come close to it. When you are consistent and accomplish your goals it is necessary for you to reward yourself, even with simple things. Accomplishing your goals will boost your confidence. Confidence plays a strong role in your ability to succeed academically and any chance you get to boost it should be taken.

Muster as much of a positive attitude as possible. It takes such an attitude to go through the numerous challenges of your coursework. Be honest with yourself and make sure you can pinpoint what works for you and what doesn't. At the end of the day your course is a bridge to your career. Building a good bridge will help you cross over properly. All your efforts will result in this. The earlier that you start preparing for the job market, the better.

Sacrifice and make the effort to attain excellent grades. As mentioned earlier, it has financial implications! In addition, doing well in school boosts one's confidence level and this is often noticed at interviews. When in need, ask for help. Make sure you ask questions in class and of other students. No one can read your mind so let the right people know the assistance that you need. You may be positively surprised at the response that you get. Reward yourself as you continue to accomplish your goals. It is important to motivate yourself. Keep these rewards simple and inexpensive. Finally, make the effort to do well academically. The lessons and experiences from attaining strong academic results will have a positive spill over into your career as well as your private life. It is worth it!

**Aim High**

"It is the working man who is the happy man. It is the idle man who is the miserable man." Benjamin Franklin

# Bibliography

Allen, David (2001). *Getting things done: the Art of Stress-Free Productivity.* New York: Viking

Anderson, J.R. (1976). *Language, Memory and Thought.* Mahwah, NJ: Erlbaum.

Cohn, Marvin (1979). *Helping Your Teen-Age Student: What Parents Can Do to Improve Reading and Study Skills,* Dutton.

Curtis, Polly (2008) *University Dropouts steady at 22%.* Guardian February 20, p. 12.

Davies, James, R. (1976). *Teaching strategies for the college classroom.* West view Press.

De Simone, Jeffrey, S. (2008) *The impact of employment during school on college student academic performance.* NBER Working Paper 14006. National Bureau of Economic Research. Cambridge, Massachusetts, May.

Dynarski, Susan, M. (2008) Building the stock of college educated labor. Journal of Human Resources 43, no. 3 (Summer) 576-610

Ebbinghaus, H. (1913). *Memory: A Contribution to Experimental Psychology,* Teacher's College, Columbia University (English edition).

Eugene M. Schwartz (1997). *How to Double Your Child's Grades in School: Build Brilliance and Leadership Into Your Child-From Kindergarten to College In Just 5 Minutes a Day,* Instant Improvement, 1997.

Fiore, Neil A (2006). *The Now Habit: A Strategic Program for Overcoming Procrastination and Enjoying Guilt- Free Play.* New York: Penguin Group.

Forster, Mark (2006-07-20). *Do It Tomorrow and Other Secrets of Time Management.* Hodder & Stoughton Religious.

Fry, Ron (2005). *How to Study.* 6th Edition, Delmar Cengage Learning, NY.

Gold, Minni. (2003) *Help for the struggling student: Ready-to-use Strategies and Resources to build attention, memory and organizational skills.* Hoboken, N.J. Jossey-Bass.

Green, Gordon, W. Jr, PhD. *Getting straight A's*. New York Lyle Staurt.

Green, Sharon (1980) *Making the grade in college*. Hauppauge, NY Barrons.

Harris, Seymour, E. (1972) *A statistical portrait of higher education*. NY McGraw-Hill.

Hubbard, L. Ron (1972). *The Management Series Volume 2, "Doing Work" chapter*. Los Angeles: Bridge Publications, Inc.

Jenson, Eric (1997*) B's and A's in 30 days*. Barrons

Jenson, Eric (1996*) Student Success Secrets*. 4th Edition. Hauppauge, NY. Barrons.

Kalat, J. W. (2001). *Biological psychology (7th ed.)*. Belmont, CA: Wadsworth Publishing.

Kornhauser, Arthur, W. (1993) How to study: Suggestions for High School and College Students. Chicago. University of Chicago Press.

Kranyik, Robert and Shankman, Florence V. (1963). *"How to Teach Study Skills"*, Teacher's Practical Press.

Lakein, Alan (1973). *How to Get Control of Your Time and Your Life*. New York: P.H. Wyden.

Langan, John (2010). *Reading and Study Skills*. 9th Edition. McGraw-Hill, New York.

Morgenstern, Julie (2004). *Time Management from the Inside Out: The Foolproof System for Taking Control of Your Schedule--and Your Life* (2nd ed.). New York: Henry Holt/Owl Books.

Organization for Economic Co-operation and Development (2002) *Education at a glance 2002: OECD Indicators* Paris: OECD.

Pelton, Ross (1989) *Mind food and smart pills*. NY Doubleday

Preston, Ralph (1959). *Teaching Study Habits and Skills*, Rinehart. Original from the University of Maryland digitized August 7, 2006.

Ravitch, Diane (1987) *The troubled crusade: American Education 1945 – 1980*. New York. Basic Books.

Richman, Howard. *"Study Methods, Study Skills, Study Tips"* (in EN). © 1998-2009 Sound Feelings Publishing, Tarzana, California.

Sandberg, Jared (2004-09-10). *"Though Time-Consuming, To-Do Lists Are a Way of Life"*. The Wall Street Journal.

U.S. Department of Education, National Center for Education Statistics: (1993*) 120 Years of American Education: A statistical portrait*. Washington D.C. U.S. Department of Education.

# Appendix 1A.
## Education Success Profile (E.S.P.)

**Instructions:**

Answer each of the following questions as truthfully as possible; then total to obtain your score.

On a scale of 1 – 10 with 1 being the lowest and 10 being the highest level possible;

1. How would you grade your reading/comprehension level?

   1…..2…..3…..4…..5…..6…..7…..8…..9…..10

2. How would you grade your writing skills level?

   1…..2…..3…..4…..5…..6…..7…..8…..9…..10

3. How would you grade your math skills level?

   1…..2…..3…..4…..5…..6…..7…..8…..9…..10

4. How would you grade your presentation skills level?

   1…..2…..3…..4…..5…..6…..7…..8…..9…..10

5. How would you grade your ability to work with other students in study groups and project works?

   1…..2…..3…..4…..5…..6…..7…..8…..9…..10

6. How would you grade your recent academic performance?

   1…..2…..3…..4…..5…..6…..7…..8…..9…..10

7. How would you grade your class attendance record?

   1…..2…..3…..4…..5…..6…..7…..8…..9…..10

8.  How would you grade your Time Management skills?

    1…..2…..3…..4…..5…..6…..7…..8…..9…..10

9.  How would you grade your note taking skills?

    1…..2…..3…..4…..5…..6…..7…..8…..9…..10

10. How would you grade your ability to understand your textbooks from your various courses?

    1…..2…..3…..4…..5…..6…..7…..8…..9…..10

**Total Score:** …………………..

**No. of areas below level 8:** ……………………

# Appendix 1B.
# Education Success Profile (E.S.P.) Interpretation

**Directions:**

Total your scores for the questions in Appendix 1a. A Total Score below 80 indicates and extra effort to enhance skills. A score of below Level 8 in 3 or more areas indicates a need for external support and guidance. Use the areas with scores below Level 8 as a guide to pay special attention to sections in the book dealing with those topics.

**Interpretation of scores:**

Include extra sessions in your study calendar for areas that you scored below 8.

If necessary, seek advice from experts to improve in these areas.

Undertake this self-assessment at the beginning and end of each semester. It will assist you to continuously improve your various academic skills.

**Specific recommended strategies for each response below Level 8:**

1. *How would you grade your reading/comprehension level?*
   **Increase reading time per day**

2. *How would you grade your writing skills level?*
   **Increase writing assignments/activity**

3. *How would you grade your math skills level?*
   **Increase math practice time per day**

4. *How would you grade your presentation skills level?*
   **Increase presentation practice**

5.  *How would you grade your ability to work with other students in study groups and project works?*
    **Identify limiting factors and make effort to be a positive team member**

6.  *How would you grade your recent academic performance?*
    **Note changes in academic performance and adjust study plan for improved performance**

7.  *How would you grade your class attendance record?*
    **Ensure you develop a strong attendance record**

8.  *How would you grade your Time Management skills?*
    **Maintain records of activity and review weekly**

9.  *How would you grade your note taking skills?*
    **Device simple shorthand**

10. *How would you grade your ability to understand your textbooks from your various courses?*
    **Increase reading time; create questions to answer after reading topics**

# Appendix 2

| TIME | MONDAY | TUESDAY | WEDNESDAY | THURSDAY | FRIDAY | SATURDAY | SUNDAY |
|---|---|---|---|---|---|---|---|
| | MIKE SMITH STUDY CALENDAR | | | | | | |
| | FALL 2019 | | LACEWOOD BUSINESS SCHOOL | | | | |
| TIME | 9AM | 9AM | 9AM | 9AM | 9AM | 9AM | 9AM |
| | CLASS BUZ LAW | CLASS MKTG | CLASS BUZ LAW | CLASS MKTG | | | |
| TIME | 11AM | 11AM | 11AM | 11AM | 11AM | 11AM | 11AM |
| | CLASS ACCOUNTING | CLASS HR | CLASS ACCOUNTING | CLASS HR | | | |
| TIME | 1PM | 1PM | 1PM | 1PM | 1PM | 1PM | 1PM |
| | STUDY GROUP A/C | STUDY GROUP A/C | STUDY GROUP LAW | STUDY GROUP A/C | | | |
| TIME | 2PM | 2PM | 2PM | 2PM | 2PM | 2PM | 2PM |
| | CLASS MGT | CLASS INT BUZ | CLASS MGT | CLASS INT BUZ | | | |
| TIME | 4PM | 4PM | 4PM | 4PM | 4PM | 4PM | 4PM |
| | REST | REST | REST | REST | REST | REST | |
| TIME | 5PM | 5PM | 5PM | 5PM | 5PM | 5PM | 5PM |
| | ASSIGNMENTS | ASSIGNMENTS | ASSIGNMENTS | ASSIGNMENTS | ASSIGNMENTS | ASSIGNMENTS | |
| TIME | 7PM | 7PM | 7PM | 7PM | 7PM | 7PM | 7PM |
| | STUDY AC | STUDY LAW | STUDY MKTG | STUDY INT BUZ | STUDY MGT | STUDY HR | |

# Appendix 3

| Sample Monthly Budget | | |
|---|---|---|
| **Monthly Net Income** | | |
| Income (1st job) | $ | 1,105 |
| Income (2nd job) | $ | 955 |
| Other Income | $ | 0 |
| **Monthly Net Income Total** | $ | 2,060 |
| | | |
| **Monthly Expenses** | | |
| Savings | $ | 100 |
| Mortgage/Rent | $ | 600 |
| Car Payment | $ | 150 |
| Car/Home Insurance | $ | 100 |
| Health Insurance | $ | 20 |
| Heating | $ | 0 |
| Cable/Phone | $ | 100 |
| Electric | $ | 90 |
| Other | $ | 100 |
| **Monthly Expenses Total** | $ | 1,260 |
| | | |
| **Monthly Spending Money** | $ | 800 |
| (*Monthly Net Income Total* minus *Monthly Expenses Total*) | | |
| | | |
| **Daily Spending Money Goal** | $ | 27 |
| (*Monthly Spending Money* divided by 30)* | | |

Printed in the United States
By Bookmasters